Women of the Bible
Volume 1

Helpmeets & Homemakers

By

Shirley M. Starr

Copyright © 2003
Shirley M. Starr
Starr Publications
Dallastown, PA

ISBN   978-0-9728162-0-5

Second Printing   November, 2010
First Printing   March, 2003

NOTE: All Bible references taken from
the Authorized Version (KJV).

Printed by

Bethel Baptist Church
4212 Campbell St.
London, Ontario, Canada N6P 1A6

(519) 652-2619
(866) 295-4143
info@bethelbaptist.ca

Dedication

This book is dedicated to
my best friend of the past thirty-five years,
my wonderful and loving husband, Randy.
His encouragement and support
made this volume possible,
including his many hours of editing.

♥ Much love and gratitude goes to him. ♥

Preface

These lessons on Bible women were taught to a handful of ladies in a home Bible study in the early 1980s by the author. After beginning the study, there was a great excitement to see what God would reveal through each new upcoming Bible lady. Later, in the mid 1990s, more studies were added and taught in our Bible Institute. What great lessons God left for us in these women of the past! How we can apply their situations and principles to our own lives even today!

Who ever hears much of anything about the women of the Bible? Not many sermons are preached on these great ladies. They suffered personal trials, tragedies, and triumphs like ladies of today. They were also women of beauty and faith, experiencing the same physical, mental, emotional, and spiritual needs we face in today's age and culture.

No matter what your current stage of life, you will be certain to find a Biblical counterpart in our study of these women. My prayer is that you will be enlightened and uplifted to see how God used these women, bearing in mind that He continues to use women today.

The Bible shows us women as daughters, wives, mothers, widows, servants, and queens. We see many different roles and character traits. John Angell James said:

> There, amidst kings, priests, warriors, and prophets, are to be seen the portraits of "the holy women of the old time, who trusted in God," as well as of those who disgraced themselves and dishonored their sex . . . In the great drama of life, as it passes before us in the Bible, no mean or inconsiderable part is assigned to female characters . . . They are a "beacon to warn us or a lamp to guide us." (James, p. 47, 59)

May you be richly blessed and challenged in your own walk with God as you learn about these helpmeets and homemakers of yesteryear.

Table of Contents

Women of the Bible, volume 1

Helpmeets & Homemakers

Title page
Copyright page
Dedication page
Preface

Sources
How to Order additional copies

Chapter 1

EVE
The First Mother

Facts

Husband:	Adam
Children:	Cain Abel Seth (others unnamed)
Occupation:	Housewife
Her name means	"life," "life-giver"

Creation and Naming   (Gen. 1:26-28, 31; 2:18-24; 3:20; 5:2)

Eve is the first lady to make her debut in God's portrait gallery of women. Her life sets a pattern for all of those who follow her. We will see that many of the problems she dealt with are the same problems we as women face today. God's love and care for her are shown throughout the Scripture just as He demonstrates His love and care to us today. We see tragedy and triumph, defeat and victory, sowing and reaping, in Eve's life.

Eve was created by God on the sixth day. God, in His compassion and mercy, saw that it was not good for Adam to be alone, that Adam needed an help meet. We see in Genesis 2:21-22 that God changed His method of creation when He created Eve. Causing a deep sleep to fall upon Adam, God took one of Adam's ribs and created the very first woman from it. It has been said that "man slept through woman's creation and she has been a puzzle to him ever since." As ladies, we know this to be very true! We are a unique creation, different not only physically, but emotionally. God knew that man needed this to balance him and make him happy.

Adam, himself, named Eve. In Genesis 2:23, he called her "woman" meaning "man-ness" or "she-man." How fitting, since she was taken from his side. Then in Genesis 3:20, we see Adam calling her "Eve" meaning "life." God also became involved in the naming process in Genesis 5:2 and called **their** name "Adam." What a beautiful picture of one flesh or unity which was His desire for this first couple!

Adam was so taken up with this delightful creature God had given him that he was inspired to write the first poem in the Bible in Genesis 2:23-24. Adam said, "This is now bone of my bones, and flesh of my flesh: she shall be called Woman, because she was taken out of Man. Therefore shall a man leave his father and his mother, and shall cleave unto his wife: and they shall be one flesh." What another beautiful picture of the marital relationship. Everything was so perfect!

God even gave them equal rule. Genesis 1:26-28 tells us that God gave **them** dominion over the fish, fowl, and every living thing. Notice that God did not give Adam dominion until Adam had Eve with him. It was a perfect setup. Life could not have been better for this first couple until . . .

Temptation and Yielding (Gen. 2:16-17; 3:1-6; 1 John 2:16)

In the midst of this perfect set-up, God had given them only one rule. He had told them not to eat from the tree of the knowledge of good and evil. Scripture shows us He dealt with Adam first about this. Genesis 2:16 says, "And the Lord God commanded the man . . ." What an important principle for us as ladies to follow, to allow the Lord to deal with our husbands first and not to take matters into our own hands!

Scripture does not reveal how Eve knew the rule. Either Adam communicated it to her, or God dealt with her, because we see later in the scenario that Eve was aware of the rule! She had no trouble with the mandate until she had her talk with the tempter. Eugenia

Price has called this, "Eve and the fatal conversation." And how fatal it did become!

As the tempter or serpent approached Eve, we see he asked for information he already knew. His method included:

1. "Is it a sin or not?"   Doubt   *(Gen.3:1)*
2. "There's no danger!"   Denial   *(Gen. 3:4)*
3. "There are advantages to it!" Discontentment *(Gen. 3:5)*

Notice the progression. Satan gets us to doubt first, then to deny, then to become discontent.

Eve's weakness was curiosity and Satan's temptation was to make her seek independence from God and from her husband. Satan attacked the weaker vessel first! Eve also added to the Scripture. In Genesis 2:17 God had instructed them not to eat of the tree. In Genesis 3:3, Eve tells the serpent they were not to eat of it or to **touch** it! Why was she making the command harder? Did she realize her weakness that if she touched it, she might be more tempted to partake?

Satan knew her weakness and tempted her in the same three ways he tempts us today. What are those three ways? We find them in 1 John 2:16. First he tempted her **physically** through her bodily appetite or the "lust of the flesh." She "saw that the tree was good for **food**."

Next he tempted her **emotionally** by appealing to her sensuous nature or the "lust of the eyes." He really likes to attack women in this area because we are such emotional creatures! Eve saw that the tree was "pleasant to the **eyes**." We need to exercise great care with what we allow into our eye gate. Soap operas, novels, wrong music, etc. all make the "grass on the other side of the fence look greener," and soon we become discontent with our own homes and marriages.

Finally he tempted her **spiritually** using the "pride of life." Eve saw that the tree was "a tree to be desired to make one **wise**." The serpent appealed to that pride, promising her she would become as a **god**, knowing good and evil. What havoc he wanted to create in her marriage and in her relationship with her God.

In Matthew 4:1-10, we see that when Satan tempted Christ in the wilderness, he used the exact same method:

> **physically** – turn stones to bread,
> **emotionally** – cast thyself down, and
> **spiritually** – fall down and worship me.

God had given Adam and Eve free choice just as He has us today. In Genesis 3:6, we see both of them yielding to the temptation. Eve took and gave to her husband. Notice that we rarely sin alone. Our sin almost always involves others, just as hers did. And our sin's consequences affect others just as hers did.

By partaking of the fruit, they disobeyed the revealed will of God, believed Satan's lie, and placed their will above God's will. What a sad day for them **and** us as their sin tainted the whole human race!

Genesis 3:6 also shows us that sin always progresses downhill. She saw; she took; she did eat; and she gave. By getting Adam to eat, we see one of the greatest tools a woman has: **the power of influence**. Every Bible woman wields this tool whether for good or for bad. How careful we as women, wives, and mothers need to be! What a dynamic weapon we have in that power of influence! Our influence can affect many for years to come.

Shame and Humiliation   (Gen. 3:7-8, 12-16, 20; John 16:21)

Adam and Eve immediately knew they had disobeyed as their eyes were opened. Opened to what? Opened to their nakedness and disgrace. Eve now became the first seamstress or dressmaker. They showed their guilt by making aprons and by hiding from the Lord. Don't we see the same principle carried out in children? When they disobey, they try to cover or hide their sin from mommy or daddy or teacher.

Helpmeets & Homemakers
Women of the Bible, volume 1

Not only did Adam and Eve try to hide or cover their sin, but they now became blame-shifters. Adam blamed Eve and partly blamed God. In Genesis 3:12, he says, "The woman **thou** gavest to be with me." Immediately, we see the disharmony sin brings into the home and marriage relationship. Then, Eve blamed the serpent saying, "the serpent beguiled me, and I did eat." Neither one wanted to face the fact or own up to their part in the sin.

Eve's whole life now changed. Genesis 3:16 reveals the three ways her life would be different. She would experience sorrow from conception, sorrow in childbirth and motherhood, and submission to her husband. No longer equal dominion! Notice how gracious our loving God is, though! The sorrow of conception and birth would be forgotten when the child is born *(John 16:21)*, and submission would be to her own husband who loved her! Even in chastening, God showed His love for her!

Their sin affected three relationships:

1. Man to God   Broken fellowship
2. Man to Man   Husband to rule wife
3. Man to Nature   Ground cursed

However, God already had a plan for redemption as shown in Genesis 3:15. We see the first promise of a Messiah, a Redeemer to break the curse and free us from sin!

Imagine the shame of being driven from the garden! There were no other people with whom to fellowship. They would no longer experience the walks and talks they had enjoyed with the Lord, would now face a cursed ground, and would work by the sweat of their brow. However, we see Adam's faith remained. In Genesis 3:20, he called the woman God had given him, "Eve" or "life-giver." Life would go on. Eve would bare children.

Marriage and Motherhood   <small>(Gen. 2:18, 22,24; 3:20; 4:1-2, 25-26; 5:3-4,24)</small>

Eve now became the first bride and Adam's wife, in the physical sense. God, the Father, gave her away. Genesis 2:22 says He "brought her unto the man." Imagine what Eve experienced! No premarital counseling, no big wedding, no guests, just her and Adam. She became pregnant with Cain. No baby showers, no "how to" books, no pre-natal classes, not even a doctor! No one had ever been pregnant before! With whom could she compare notes? And what about morning sickness? What did she think as the womb began to grow and she first felt life? Joyce Landorf describes it well:

> "At first she was mystified by the changes in her swollen body, fearful of the unknown and terrified of the actual pain of childbearing itself. But, after she had lived through fifty or sixty birthing experiences, it was only the pain she could never properly prepare herself to endure, nor strangely enough, remember when it was over."
> *(Landorf, p. 28)*

Cain was Eve's first son and she recognized the hand of the Lord in this as she said in Genesis 4:1 "I have gotten a man from the Lord." Imagine the thrill she felt holding the very first baby ever in her arms! Little did she know what sorrow she would face through that grown child. Later Abel was born and Cain grew to hate him as Abel's heart was directed toward the things of God and Cain's was not.

Think of the sorrow Eve faced when Cain killed Abel. What a turmoil prevailed in their home and all because of sin. Eve faced the death of a son with no available support group. The first murder was committed and directly within her own household! Imagine her grief with her oldest son, a murderer, and her youngest son, the victim! She undoubtedly dealt with great anger toward Cain and inconsolable grief concerning Abel. She may even have felt the guilt of sowing and reaping for disobeying the Lord in the garden and taking of the forbidden fruit. The first funeral occurred with no pastor or friends to comfort her. It was a sad day, indeed!

Perhaps you have experienced or are experiencing a mountain of grief in your own life. Are you grieving over the loss of a child, a wayward child, or a broken home? Be not dismayed! Help is just around the corner as it was with Eve. God will not put more upon you than you can bear *(1 Cor. 10:13)*. Likewise, He knew Eve's "load limit."

Once again, God again demonstrated His love and mercy to her by sending Seth, the son who would produce a Godly generation. God was so gracious to give her Seth who would soothe her aching heart over the great loss of Abel. Scripture tells us Eve had many other sons and daughters. *(Gen. 5:4)*

Eve was to experience yet more joy when she became a grandmother to Enoch, the one who "walked with God: and he was not; for God took him." *(Gen. 5:24)* She is often called "the mother of mankind," "the mother of all living," "and the mother of all dying."

Conclusions   (2 Cor. 11:3; 1 Tim. 2:14)

There is no record of Eve's death in the Bible. The New Testament does mention Eve, verifying even more the events in Genesis. We are cautioned in 2 Corinthians 11:3 not to be beguiled as Eve was; to keep our minds on the "simplicity that is in Christ."

Eve was the first to experience marriage, pregnancy, childbirth, motherhood, grand-motherhood, a wayward son, and the death of a son. She had no other lady with whom to share and was a mother who had never been a child herself. How did she do it? Perhaps she remembered the walks with the Lord in the garden. What other lady was so privileged to walk with the Lord? She knew God loved her as He always demonstrated His mercy and compassion to her.

She faced many things that we as women face today, such as temptation, sin, disappointment, sorrow. Through Eve's life, we can gain courage to go through our own trials of life, knowing that there is a God of compassion and mercy Who loves us very much. How important it is to maintain our own walk with the Lord so we do not face the shame and humiliation that Eve did. If shame and humiliation have come into our lives through sin, though, we have a merciful, compassionate, loving, and forgiving God. How important to wield our power of influence in the correct manner as it touches the lives of our families, co-workers, and friends.

Eve's Roles

1. Helpmeet
2. Companion
3. Wife
4. Mother
5. Grandmother
6. Counselor
7. Homemaker
8. Seamstress

Eve's Character Traits

1. Impulsiveness
2. Curiosity
3. Greediness
4. Blame-shifting
5. Head-strong

Chapter 2

SARAH

The First Missionary Wife

Facts

Husband:	Abram (Abraham)
Children:	Isaac
Occupation:	Housewife
Her name means:	"princess," "mother of nations"

Marriage (Gen. 11:29-31)

Sarai was the wife of Abram and lived in Ur, a well-developed, civilized community. She was a "city gal," and accustomed to luxury and a rich life style. How do we know this? John R. Rice in his commentary on Genesis describes the homes, commerce, and education in Ur. He tells us the average middle class home usually had from 10-20 rooms. Ur was a great city of trade with imports of "copper, ore, gold, ivory, hard woods, . . ." The people had academic skills in arithmetic, reading, and writing. So, we see that Sarai was used to the city life and probably had servants and wealth at her disposal. Perhaps she was accustomed to culture and entertainment. Little did she know how her life was going to change!

Missionary (Gen. 11:31; 12:1-8; Acts 7:2-4; Eph. 5:23; 1 Pet. 3:6)

Sarah became the first missionary wife. Abram was called to the mission field while in Ur. Notice the Lord again dealt with the husband first as in the case of Adam. "Now the Lord had said unto

Abram . . ." *(Gen. 12:1)* How would they leave the luxuries of Ur to go to a place they knew not of? – a place that the Lord would show them? What were Sarai's thoughts? Perhaps she thought, "Wow, I am getting pretty old for this kind of thing. After all, 65 is not a young age to be moving!" "Will Abram know the Lord's voice about where we are to settle down?" She had to have faith in her husband's walk with God. What did she have to do to get ready? She would be saying goodbye to all the family and friends she had ever known. And what about the luxuries? Was it hard to leave those? Scripture does not tell us of her feelings, only that she followed her husband. What an example to us of willingness and submission.

"So, Abram departed . . ." His nephew, Lot, and his father, Terah, were with them. They traveled from Ur and stopped at Haran on their way to Canaan. *(Acts 7:3-4)* This could be likened to deputation. Why did they stop? Perhaps Terah had become so ill he could no longer travel as we know he died there. They faced their first discouragement on the road. However, it did not hinder them and they continued on from Haran to Canaan, Abram being 75 years old. The Bible states they gained souls in Haran.

Imagine Sarai's feelings! Her house was now a drafty tent instead of a 10-20 room mansion. She faced the weariness of constant travel, dust, and dirt. Having no fellowship with other women, perhaps she became quite lonely. Only her loving relationship with her husband and her close walk with the Lord kept her going. What a culture shock this may have been for her after living in Ur! Yet, she seemed willing to face hardship without complaining and was even an encourager to Abram just by following alongside. 1 Peter 3:6 commends her for her submission and obedience.

Maintaining their walk with the Lord was important to them. Family worship was a main priority as Abram erected an altar at Bethel and "called upon the name of the Lord." *(Gen. 12:8)* They would need this spiritual strength for the trial to come.

Egypt

(Gen. 12:10-20)

There was a great famine and poverty in the land. The Bible calls it a "grievous" famine. Not seeking God's will in the matter, Abram stepped out and left the promised land for Egypt, probably seeking food and hoping to better provide for his family. Sarai was so beautiful that he instructed her to tell a half- truth and tell others that she was his sister. Actually, she **was** his half-sister *(Gen. 20:12)* He feared he might be killed and they would take her. Pharaoh did take her into his house and treated her well. What were her feelings at this time? Was she fearful? Was she angry toward Abram? Perhaps she was a tinge prideful that other men would notice her beauty. Just think, she was 65 years old and still had physical beauty. We can only speculate.

One thing we do know, however, is that God took care of her, even though they were out of His will. He sent great plagues unto Pharaoh's household. We do not see God appearing to Abram during this time in Egypt, though He did protect them.

When they stepped out of God's will and sinned, one sin led to another. They did not seek God; they stopped in Haran; they went to Egypt; they lied. We remember this same downhill progression with Eve—she saw; she took; she ate; she gave. Like Adam and Eve, Abram and Sarai paid dearly for this later.

Barrenness

(Gen. 11:30; 16:1-6)

The main burden Sarai carried in life was her barrenness. In Bible days, a woman was not important until she bore a son. The custom was that if a wife could not bear a son, she would find a concubine or handmaid who could. The child then was legally hers. Imagine the disappointment and sorrow over being barren! It was a disgrace! Sarai was unselfish and loved Abram so much that she was willing to give him Hagar, her Egyptian handmaid. It is likely that they had taken on this servant when they went to

Egypt. Here is another example of the well-stated phrase, "They got what they wanted, but lost what they had." By doing this, she took matters into her own hands and stepped out of God's will. She was willing to follow the customs of the day instead of God's promise for their lives. This was a great sin of disobedience and presumption. When we are out of the will of God, we may make decisions that will haunt us for years to come.

By getting Abram to take Hagar, she showed her power of influence. Genesis 16:2 tells us " . . . And Abram hearkened." (Sound familiar? Adam hearkened to Eve.) Neither one of them sought God as they made these quick decisions. Sarai used her power of influence in a wrong way and took matters into her own hands. She showed her impatience by running ahead of God, and then did not want to accept the consequences. Sin brought great turmoil in the home that continues to this day in the conflict between the Arabs (from Hagar-Ishmael) and the Israelis (from Sarai-Isaac). Be careful with that power of influence!

Jealousy overtook her when Hagar conceived and like Eve, she became a blame-shifter and told Abram, "My wrong be upon thee: . . ." *(Gen. 16:5)* Abram made her take responsibility for her decision and handle the situation. However, she was unkind toward Hagar, allowing her emotions to rule. Becoming irrational, the Bible tells us she "dealt hardly" with Hagar and Hagar fled. What a warning this should be to us to avoid making decisions based upon our emotions and taking things into our own hands!

Psalm 62:5 tells us, "Wait thou only upon God; for my expectation is from him." Often we become impatient and upset when our husbands or friends do not meet our expectations, so we think we will help them out. There goes that misused power of influence again! Seek the Lord first and you will save yourself and your family untold confusion.

Name Change
(Gen. 17:1-5, 15-19)

God continued to reveal Himself to Abram and promised to give him seed even though he was 99 years old now! It was during this time that God changed Abram's name to Abraham and Sarai's name to Sarah, meaning "princess." Again, God dealt with Abraham first concerning the promise of a son. Abraham laughed and asked how a hundred year old man and ninety year old woman could conceive? God even told him what they were to name the child – Isaac, meaning "laughter." God promised them a son thirteen (13) times in Genesis and told Abraham that Sarah would be a "mother of nations," and that "kings of people" would come from her. No wonder the natural man would laugh! God's ways are not our ways! Even though they had run ahead of God's perfect will for their lives, God continued to remind them of His promise and demonstrate His love to them.

Hospitality
(Gen. 18:1-15; 1 Tim. 3:2; Heb. 13:2)

As the story progresses, we find Sarah being the first woman to use hospitality. She kept everything simple, unlike her days in Ur. Now she had no servants to help. She had simple accommodations, a tent. She had simple food; cakes, butter, milk, beef. And there was simple enjoyment. Cooking for three unexpected guests, Abraham and Sarah worked together. She did not have time to clean the tent or plan the menu. These unexpected guests caused them to hurry in their preparation to serve them ("hastened" and "ran" in *Gen. 18:6-7).*

The Bible encourages this hospitality in Hebrews 13:2 when it says not to be "forgetful to entertain strangers: for thereby some have entertained angels unawares." Her unexpected guests even knew her name and repeated the promise to Abraham of having a son. How did Sarah react to their visit? She laughed and was sarcastic and unbelieving. "How could a 90 year old woman have a son!" Besides God had been saying this for 25 years! Wouldn't you give up after 25 years? God promised them a physical miracle saying He would return unto them "according to the time of life" and she **would** have a son.

Gerar   (Gen. 20:1-8; 14-16)

Abraham continued on his deputation trip and journeyed south to Gerar. As if he did not learn his lesson the first time around, he lied again saying that Sarah was his sister. The king of Gerar, Abimelech, sent for Sarah and took her. Why would he want a 90 year-old woman? Maybe the miracle was already beginning to take place! Perhaps Sarah was in her second youth, with her beauty restored. God protected her again by appearing to Abimelech in a dream. (Remember the last time He had used plagues.) Abimelech returned Sarah with cattle, servants, and 1,000 pieces of silver. The Scripture says Sarah was reproved, Abraham was to be her covering, and she was not to look at other men. What godly advice for us as women to follow today! Our husbands are to be our covering and we are not to be looking at or seeking attention from other men.

Miracle Birth   (Gen. 21:1-8; Rom. 4:19; Heb. 11:11)

God's promise was about to be fulfilled! Part of the miracle was the restoration of youth to Abraham and Sarah so they could conceive. Sarah did conceive and bore a son! God always keeps His promises! Can you imagine the excitement and joy in this home?

Abraham named the boy Isaac and circumcised him. Sarah's laugh was no longer one of sarcasm, but one of pure joy and delight! The Bible even cites proofs of the miracle:

1. Her womb had been dead. She had already gone through

menopause. *(Rom. 4:19)*
2. God restored her strength to conceive and deliver.
   A 90 year old woman going through labor and
   delivery? *(Heb. 11:11)*
3. She **nursed** the babe. A 90 year-old woman nursing a
   child? *(Gen. 21:7-8)*

Hagar   (Gen. 21:9-13; Gal. 4:22-31)

Once again, jealousy poked its ugly head into the joyful
occasion. Sarah continued to reap for her earlier sin of
disobedience. She happened to see Ishmael, the child of Hagar,
mocking Isaac. If Isaac was about three to five (3-5) years old,
then Ishmael was 17-19. She approached Abraham asking him to
cast Hagar and her son out of the family. Abraham was grief-
stricken, but God comforted him and told him to listen to Sarah
this time. He also promised Abraham that a nation would come
out of Ishmael's seed. Abraham cast Hagar out, symbolizing the
old covenant replaced by the new; law replaced by grace; and the
bondwoman versus the free woman.

Death and Burial   (Gen. 23:1-2; 19-20; 24:67)

God was gracious to Sarah and gave her 37 years to see Isaac
grow up. She was 90 at his birth and 127 when she died. She is
the only Bible woman whose age is listed at her death. Abraham
mourned greatly for her and buried her in a cave at Machpelah.
This is the first grave mentioned in Scripture. Her legacy, like
Eve's, carries over into the New Testament as she is mentioned in
Romans 4:19, 9:9 and Hebrews 11:11, God's hall of faith. What a
love story God portrayed for us!

Lessons from Sarah   (Psa. 106:15)

Sarah was willing to follow her husband anywhere. Her relationship with Abraham pictures the relationship of Christ and the Church. She stood behind her husband in spite of his mistakes. What a great love affair they had! We see God dealing with Abraham, the head of the home first on several occasions. What a challenge this is to us as wives to be in total submission to our husbands and to allow God to deal with them instead of playing God ourselves.

We also learn that it does not pay to make quick decisions without seeking God, although He often still protects us when we are out of His will. Often we slow down what God wants to do in our lives because we step out of His will and try to rush things or avoid things. Like Eve, Sarah made decisions based on her emotions and they turned out to be poor decisions. In these ladies we see a pattern developing which is a forewarning to us not to make a decision when we are emotionally upset.

If we do not learn a lesson the first time, we may have to repeat the experience until we do. So it was with Abraham, Sarah, and the lying.

Sarah used her power of influence in the wrong manner, making life miserable for Abraham, herself, and Hagar. The consequences of that action carried down through the years. God will often let us have our way, but there is a price to pay. We may not reap what we sow right away; it could be years down the road. We may "get what we want, but lose what we have."

Lastly, we see that God is the God of miracles and always keeps His promises in our lives. However, His timing is not our timing. Abraham and Sarah waited 25 years until the promise was fulfilled.

Helpmeets & Homemakers
Women of the Bible, volume 1

Sarah's Roles

1. Wife
2. Mother
3. Servant
4. Missionary
5. Hostess

Sarah's Character Traits

1. Unselfishness
2. Submissiveness
3. Flexibility
4. Faithfulness
5. Outspokenness
6. Obstinacy
7. Impatience
8. Hospitable
9. Jealousy
10. Doubt

NOTES:

Chapter 3

RACHEL, LEAH
The Competitive Women

Facts – Rachel

Husband:	Jacob
Children:	Joseph, Benjamin
Occupation:	Housewife
Her name means:	"ewe," "little lamb"

Facts - Leah

Husband:	Jacob
Children:	Reuben, Simeon, Levi, Judah, Issachar, Zebulun, Dinah
Occupation:	Housewife
Her name means	"wearied," "faint from sickness"

Rachel Meets Jacob   (Gen. 29:1-12, 18-20)

God saw fit to give us another Biblical romance. However, this time, it involves a triangle love affair causing much turmoil in the home between two sisters, Rachel and Leah.

Jacob had to flee his home because of his brother Esau's desire to kill him for stealing Esau's rightful blessing from Isaac. Imagine the loneliness and emotional state Jacob was in at this time! He met up with some shepherds and asked them if they knew Laban, Nahor's son. They said they did and told him Laban's daughter, Rachel, was coming with the sheep. Evidently she was a shepherdess. Rachel was the youngest daughter of

Laban and "beautiful and well favoured." *(Gen. 29:17)* Could she have been a little spoiled? Again, "a routine event" became part of a "divine plan." Rachel was just going about her daily responsibilities, little realizing how God would order her day.

As she approached the well, Jacob rolled the stone away from the mouth of the well and watered the flock for Rachel like his mother had done for Eliezer. It seemed to be love at first sight! "And Jacob kissed Rachel, and lifted up his voice, and wept." *(Gen. 29:11)* What an emotional meeting! Rachel ran home and told her father about the meeting.

Leah's Characteristics   (Genesis 29:16-17; 1 Sam. 16:7)

Leah was Laban's oldest daughter. The Bible describes her as "tender-eyed," having weak eyes making her less beautiful than her younger sister, Rachel. Her eyes lacked luster and perhaps she had poor sight. She seems to have had an inner beauty, though, as throughout the Biblical account, we see her maintaining a meek, submissive spirit. Was she often compared to Rachel and less favoured among family and friends?

The Deception   (Gen. 29:13-30; Gal. 6:7)

As the story continues, Jacob went to Rachel's home and met Laban. Laban gave him a hearty and warm welcome and Jacob stayed there a month. After working for Laban through that period of time, Laban asked Jacob what he could pay him for his labor. Jacob loved Rachel so much that he said he would work seven more years for her. He is considered the most devoted lover in the Bible. Jacob did not know he was going to be deceived like he had deceived Isaac and Esau. The sowing and reaping principle found in Galatians 6:7 was about to go into effect.

After seven years of hard labor, the wedding was about to take place. The custom was to conduct the bride to the bedchambers in silence and darkness. The wedding festivities usually lasted a week. *(Gen. 29:27)* It was also a custom to give the daughter a maid as a wedding gift. Leah would receive Zilpah and Rachel would receive Bilhah.

Imagine Jacob's anticipation! He had waited seven long years for the woman he loved. It had been a long wait! At the last minute, Laban tricked Jacob, switching Rachel for Leah. "Jacob, the deceiver, reaped deception." *(Ryrie, p. 53)* He never knew he had been deceived until the next morning. When he asked Laban why he had beguiled him, Laban's excuse was that the law stated the oldest daughter must be married first. Why hadn't he been honest with Jacob from the beginning? Matthew Henry comments that there probably was no such custom and that Laban was probably mocking Jacob. Because of this deception, Laban drew Jacob into polygamy. He connived for Jacob to serve seven more years for Rachel! Picture Jacob's dismay and heartbreak! Laban and Leah had both sinned in the matter.

Where was Rachel in this plot of deception or did she even know anything about it? Why didn't she speak out? Did she love Jacob as much as he loved her? Why did Leah go along with the deed – merely to obey? Maybe she had a desire to get married and had secretly loved Jacob all along.

Jacob took Rachel as his wife and then served seven more years. *(Gen. 29:27)* All in all, he worked fourteen (14) years for Rachel. How would you feel after being married a week and then your husband marries your sister? Imagine knowing that he loved your sister and not you! The stage was set for bitterness, competition, and turmoil.

Leah's Motherhood   (Gen. 29:31-35; 1 Cor. 12:24)

God has a way of balancing things. He extended mercy to the rejected Leah. "And when the Lord saw that Leah was hated, he opened her womb. . ." *(Gen. 29:31)* Her motherhood was:

Helpmeets & Homemakers
Women of the Bible, volume 1

1. A **rebuke** to Jacob for favoritism.
2. A **check** to Rachel for her gloating.
3. A **comfort** to Leah.   *(1 Cor. 12:24)*

Imagine Leah's excitement over the pregnancy!   Perhaps she thought, "Maybe Jacob will love me after I give him a son."   Four sons later she was still thinking the same thing.   Her names for her sons show her faith in God.

1. Reuben - "Behold a son"   *(Gen. 29:32)*
2. Simeon - "Hearing"   *(Gen. 29:33)*
3. Levi   - "Joined"   *(Gen. 29:34)*
4. Judah   - "Praise"   *(Gen. 29:35)*

Each time she went through the agony of labor and childbirth, she thought it would awaken Jacob's love for her.   After bearing Reuben, she said the Lord had looked upon her affliction and now Jacob would love her.   After bearing Simeon, she said the Lord knew she was hated.   After having Levi, she thought surely this time her husband would be "joined" unto her.   Praising the Lord for having Judah, she finally left it in God's hands.

Leah was a loyal wife and a good mother.   We never see her reproaching Jacob for his lack of love.   She respected him and showed it.   She seemed content even amidst her trials.   Could you be content with your sister married to your husband?

Scripture shows us her spiritual sensitivity:

1. The **Lord** hath looked.   *(Gen. 29:32)*
2. The **Lord** hath heard.   *(Gen. 29:33)*
3. I will praise the **Lord**.   *(Gen. 29:35)*

It seems she meditated on the Lord and had close fellowship with Him.   God used sorrow as an instrument in her life, causing her to become a building stone for the house of Israel, as Christ's lineage came through the tribe of Judah.   Perhaps He has used or is using that same surgical instrument on you.   Consider Leah and do not become bitter over grief and sorrow. God wants to better equip you to help others in their time of grief and suffering. *(2 Cor. 1:4-5)* Who knows how God will use your sorrow to His glory?

Rachel's Barrenness (Gen. 29:31; 30:1-8)

We see Rachel's true spirit about to be revealed. The Lord gave Leah children, "but Rachel was barren." Rachel could not control her jealousy. She became discontent and impatient and railed at Jacob, "Give me children, or else I die." *(Gen. 30:1)* Since he was obviously not sterile, either he was ignoring her (unlikely since she was beautiful) or she was deflecting blame for her barrenness and acting on her emotions. Was this perhaps a suicide threat? Or was she just speaking in the heat of the moment? She expected something out of love.

Let's compare Rachel to Hannah. Rachel became jealous and accused her husband. Hannah wept and sought God. Rachel gave orders and died. Hannah had four more children and lived.

Rachel cried out to Jacob instead of to God. Jacob became very angry and asked, "Am I God?" *(Gen. 30:2)* What did Rachel expect him to do? Rachel pouted, and became peevish and petulant, like Rebekah, and started taking matters into her own hands. Showing her self-will, she gave her handmaid Bilhah to Jacob. This reminds us of Sarah and Hagar. "I'll solve this problem myself." She was running ahead of God!

Bilhah had two sons: Dan ("God has given judgment") and Naphtali ("Wrestling"). Notice Rachel's prideful attitude here. She said she had wrestled with Leah and **she, Rachel,** had prevailed. Unlike Leah, she shows no spiritual sensitivity. She had prevailed, not God. What a sad testimony to her inner spirit (lack of inner beauty)! The Jacob home was filled with envy, anger, and bitterness.

The Competition (Gen. 30:9-21; Prov. 21:9; 25:24)

Imagine Rachel listening to Leah's babies. Leah could get revenge in Rachel's barrenness. Imagine Leah knowing Jacob loved Rachel more. Rachel could taunt Leah about not having Jacob's love. "Leah had the keys of Jacob's house, Rachel the keys of Jacob's heart." *(Matheson, p. 119)* What a pitiful situation! It was a situation bent on destroying the home!

Leah finally reacted and gave her handmaid Zilpah to Jacob. She was not about to be outdone by Rachel. Two more sons, Gad and Asher, were born to this union.

Rachel connived another method, once again trying to solve the problem herself. She coveted mandrakes, a narcotic plant, the size of a plum, known also as "love apples." These were considered to be a love charm able to open a lady's womb. *(Gen. 30:14)* And once again she did not call upon God. She manipulated people and "distributed love like merchandise." She promised Leah that Jacob would spend the night with her if Leah would give her the mandrakes Reuben had brought home. She could focus only on **her** problem and she was willing to use her own husband to get what she wanted. What a warning this is to us to beware of our emotional focus! Leah was even becoming bitter now! The stress was taking its toll on all involved. The trick backfired when Leah conceived and bore Jacob a fifth son, Issachar!

Imagine Jacob's feelings in this house of bickering and turmoil. He was a pawn. Proverbs tells us it is better to dwell on a housetop than with a brawling woman! How about having **two** brawling women in a house? Leah and Rachel had become more concerned with their reputation of childbearing than with reason or religion!

Leah bore another son, Zebulun, and a daughter, Dinah. Poor Leah! She was always trying to win her husband's love.

Rachel's Motherhood (Gen. 30:22-24)

Even though Rachel sinned, God remembered her and opened her womb. Did she finally call upon Him? It was not the mandrakes. God " . . .hearkened unto her." *(Gen. 30:22)* The Scripture says He **remembered**, He **hearkened** to her, and He **opened** her womb. What a merciful, loving, compassionate God we have! Even when we have treated Him the worst, He still comes on the scene for us! God has His perfect timing. Matthew Henry says, "He corrects our folly, considers our frame, and does not contend forever."

Rachel bore Joseph. Imagine the excitement in the home! What was her attitude? Was it one of triumph over Leah or gratefulness to the Lord? She seems to be grateful as she said the Lord had taken away her reproach. Demonstrating more faith, she said, "The Lord shall add to me another son." *(Gen. 30:24)*

Rachel's Theft (Gen. 31:4-35; 35:4)

After all these happenings, Jacob realized that Laban's attitude toward him had changed. Laban was using Jacob and cheating him. Jacob became upset after Laban changed his wages ten times. This situation seemed to unite Rachel and Leah. All of a sudden, they had a common cause, their inheritance! Notice it is something material that brought them together. They realized that Laban had not only cheated their husband, Jacob, but he had also devoured their inheritance. They planned as a family to go back to the land of Canaan to Isaac.

It is at this time that Rachel took the family images and put them in the camel's backpack and sat upon it. Why did she steal? What did the images mean to her?

1. Was she superstitious? Were they to insure a good journey or to guarantee fertility?
2. Were they pretty figurines that she wanted to keep?

3. Were they tied in with her inheritance?
4. Was she involved in religious polygamy?

It seems there was no true worship in the home. We do not see her and Jacob communicating about godly things. Her sin of theft led to the sin of lying. Three days later Laban went searching for them. Evidently the images were important to him also. Rachel told him she could not get up because the "custom of women" was upon her. The images were securely hidden! Later, Jacob got rid of all the idols. When did he find out she had them? "Be sure your sin will find you out." *(Num. 32:23)*

Rachel's Tragic Death   <small>(Gen. 35:16-20; 48:7; Ruth 4:11; Jer. 31:15; Matt 2:16-18)</small>

Rachel became pregnant again and had very hard labour. She was the first woman to die in childbirth while bearing Benjamin. She never was able to meet her father-in-law, Isaac, or to raise her baby, Benjamin. She was buried in Ephrath. This was the first pillar used to mark a grave and is the oldest memorial to a Bible woman with the grave still marked today. The Bible portrays her in sorrow. She is used in symbolism. *(Jer. 31:5, Ruth 4:11)* Once again we see an Old Testament woman mentioned in the New Testament, likened to the women weeping for their children who were killed under Herod's reign. *(Matt. 2:16-18)* Rachel had a great beginning, but a sad ending.

Leah's Death and Burial   <small>(Gen. 49:31; 50:13)</small>

No more is heard in Scripture of Leah except that she was buried in the family tomb at Machpelah alongside Abraham and Sarah, and Isaac and Rebekah. It is interesting that Jacob was buried with her and not with his favorite wife, Rachel. Had he grown to love Leah after Rachel's death?

Conclusions

Rachel was attractive on the outside but disappointing on the inside. Remember the old adage, "beauty is as beauty does?" Outward actions betray what is in our heart. ". . .for out of the abundance of the heart the mouth speaketh." *(Matt. 12:34b)* We learned about the condition of Rachel's heart during her trial of barrenness and her theft of the images. She handled life's trials poorly and refused to build her faith. How about you? How are you handling life's trials? What is on your lips coming out of the abundance of your heart?

Rachel also displayed an independence from God and her husband in wanting to govern her own life. She took matters into her own hands and became conniving and manipulative. Do you seek God before making important decisions? Do you ask your husband for advice or do you just independently make decisions without him? We can bring great difficulties into our homes by not seeking our husband's counsel. "Maxing-out" the credit card can bring financial woes. Making schedule commitments before checking with him or not taking time to talk and share can cause communication breakdown. Not spending time together can make love wax cold. How independent is your relationship? Do you have his/her checkbooks? His/her vacations? Are you always running around with "the girls?" Are you under your husband, the authority God has ordained for the home? Rachel had problems in this area.

Rachel had beauty and Jacob's love and security, but was still discontent and spiritually insensitive. How easy it is to become discontent when we are not walking close with the Lord! Paul said he had learned in whatsoever state he was to be content. *(Phil. 4:11)* Hebrews 13:5 says, ". . .and be content with such things as ye have. . ." Often we make our husbands feel like failures because we are not content with what they provide for us. We are not content with the things we have. Look around today and count your blessings! Be content with what you have!

Leah was the woman with the unhappy marriage, yet she was meek, quiet, and spiritually sensitive. She did not complain and demonstrated that suffering produces character. Perhaps her hardships kept her closer to the Lord, relying more upon Him. The only time we see her stepping out of bounds was when she followed the worldly way of Rachel and gave her handmaid to Jacob. She also connived with Rachel for the mandrakes and access to one more time of Jacob's love. If you are facing suffering in your life, use it to become closer to the Lord and dig into His promises for comfort. Memorize and meditate on the Scriptures and God will use you to help others with their suffering.

Lessons

We learn many lessons from our story of Rachel and Leah. May we apply these to our lives to be better Christian ladies, wives, and mothers.

1. We need to teach our children that inward beauty is more important and warn them to look for this when choosing a mate.
2. We need to beware of discontentment.
3. God is gracious even when we are selfish.
4. God can use an unbearable situation in our lives through which to channel blessings.
5. We cannot expect to win a partner's love **after** the wedding vows or get them saved **after** we marry them. This is disobedience to God's command not to be unequally yoked. It is the sin of presumption.
6. We learn God's wisdom in monogamous marriage.
7. God brought good out of all. Jacob had twelve sons from from which the twelve tribes of Israel descended.

Helpmeets & Homemakers
Women of the Bible, volume 1

Rachel's Roles

1. Wife
2. Mother
3. Bully
4. Thief
5. Liar
6. Conniver
7. Manipulator
8. Shepherdess

Rachel's Character Traits

1. Impatience
2. Outspokenness
3. Discontentment
4. Ungratefulness
5. Jealousy
6. Bitterness
7. Spiritual insensitivity
8. Selfishness

Leah's Roles

1. Substitute bride
2. Mother

Leah's Character Traits

1. Meekness
2. Jealousy
3. Submissiveness
4. Gentleness
5. Spiritual sensitivity

NOTES:

Chapter 4

JOCHEBED
The Woman of Faith

"The Woman Whose Children Became Great"
(Lockyer, p. 79)

Facts	
Husband:	Amram
Children:	Aaron, Moses, Miriam
Occupation:	Housewife, Nursemaid
Her name means:	"Glory of Jehovah,"
	"Jehovah is her glory"

Family and Background   (Exod. 1:13-14, 22; 6:20; Num. 26:59)

Jochebed's name means "glory of Jehovah," or "Jehovah is her glory." She is the first person in Scripture to have her name linked with Jehovah and is only mentioned by that name twice.

She was the daughter of Levi, the wife of Amram, and considered one of the most immortal mothers of Israel. The Bible tells us nothing about her physical appearance or beauty. We do know she lived under extremely difficult conditions. The Israelites were under bondage in Egypt. They were Pharaoh's slaves and suffered much hard labor and sorrow. Pharaoh became jealous of them and felt his kingdom was threatened, so he issued a law to kill all baby boys when they were born.

Jochebed was with child at this time. Imagine her anxiety and suspense! Although she had two other children, Aaron and Miriam, her mother's heart was not willing to see this babe sacrificed! No ultrasound would reveal whether this child were a boy or girl. She had to wait out the whole nine-month period to find out! Did she seek God during this time and pray a hedge around her baby? *(Job 1:10)*

Motherhood

(Exodus 1:16-20; 2:2; Num. 26:59; Acts 7:20; Heb. 11:23)

The Lord intervened and touched the hearts of the Hebrew midwives and they refused to obey the Pharaoh's command, fearing the Lord. They saved the baby boys and Scripture tells us that God blessed them for doing it.

Jochebed's day of delivery came and she brought forth a son. Imagine her mixed feelings of joy and fear! A baby boy? But how could she protect him? She must have already been thinking of a plan.

What were her feelings about her infant, Moses? The Bible says she saw that "he was a goodly child." Perhaps she recognized he was destined for a special purpose. Maybe like Mary she pondered this in her heart. She suppressed her maternal love and dedicated her son to God, though she knew he would not grow up in her home.

Scripture tells us three different times that there was something special about Moses. Exodus 2:2 says he was a "goodly child." He was of good or fine appearance, a perfect little baby boy! Acts 7:20 tells us he was "exceeding fair," meaning he had a pleasing appearance and was free from blemish. And Hebrews 11:23 says he was a "proper child," meaning "comely, elegant of body, fair."

Jochebed was determined to save this child. She managed to hide him for three months in her home. How did she keep him quiet? She probably had to instruct Aaron and Miriam not to tell their friends. She was a fighter and would not let her baby be thrown to the crocodiles. She hazarded her own life to save her son. Hebrews 11:23 tells us Moses' parents were not afraid of Pharaoh's edict. Oh, that there were more mothers today with this same resolve not to let the world and Satan get their children! We mothers need to be determined like Jochebed and seek God on behalf of our children.

The Plan   (Exod. 2:3-10; 7:15; 8:20)

Moses was three months old and getting noisier and noisier. What could she do? She came up with a plan that showed much faith mixed with wisdom. She did not become a victim of her emotions or live in fear. Being creative, she made an ark, a little basket or boat made out of papyrus reed that grew in the marshes along the Nile River. Then, after daubing the ark with pitch, she had faith to put the baby in it. Do you think her faith wavered? Of the different types of crocodiles in the world, one is called the Nile crocodile and unique to this area *(World Book, "Nile")*. Would you be willing to put your baby into a basket and float it in a crocodile-infested river? Jochebed trusted God.

After putting the baby in the river, she instructed Miriam to watch over the ark. Once again we see her teaching. She probably knew Pharaoh's daughter bathed every day at a certain place. "A routine event became part of a divine plan" again. Jochebed put action to her faith - nothing ventured, nothing gained. She did not wait for others to work out the problem for her or run around the neighborhood asking what everyone else would do. God gave her a plan and she carried it out!

The princess, right on schedule, came down to bathe. She saw the ark and sent her maid to fetch it. After opening the basket and seeing the child, her heart was filled with compassion. Had Jochebed counted on this maternal instinct?

Miriam fulfilled her part in the plan. Jochebed had probably trained her in the exact words to say. Miriam asked the princess if she wanted her to go and find a nurse for the baby. Pharaoh's daughter agreed to the plan! Imagine Jochebed's joy when Miriam ran home and told her the good news! Jochebed hastened off to see the princess, knowing she would soon be holding her baby in her arms again! The princess even agreed to pay her for nursing the child! Because of this, Jochebed was able to guide the formative years of her son, Moses. God in His providence had worked a miracle and supplied mercy.

Moses grew and soon it was time to wean him and take him to Pharaoh's daughter. How Jochebed's heart probably yearned to see him grow up! However, like Hannah, she knew she had to dedicate him to the Lord's work and let go. Are you willing to dedicate your child to the Lord's work? Are you willing to let go if God would call your child to a special ministry?

Influence On Her Children

We see the great influence Jochebed must have had on her three children as all of them became great:

1. Moses was the greatest national leader and legislator the world has ever known and wrote the five books of the law.

2. Aaron became the first high priest and overseer of the Aaronic priesthood and functioned as a second man.

3. Miriam was the first prophetess, a poetess, and a musician.

Jochebed apparently transferred good character to her children, though we see in later years that they were not perfect either. This shows us the influence a mother has on her children and the importance of their formative years. Although she only had Moses in her care for a short period of time, in later years he did not yield to Egyptian influence.

Conclusions

(Prov. 22:1; Eccl. 7:1; Heb. 11:23)

Jochebed, like several other Bible women studied so far, is mentioned in the New Testament. We see from Hebrews 11:23 that she and Amram, her husband, worked together on hiding Moses. Perhaps she sought Amram's counsel about the plan of the ark. She showed imagination, creativity, and common sense, besides being poised, clever, balanced, and self-controlled. She was not a victim of her emotions. Often women will say, "Well, I made a bad decision because I was so emotional!" This was not so with Jochebed. She evidently had a close walk with the Lord and was a Spirit-controlled woman as she did not become hysterical and fall apart in a life-threatening situation. Knowing where to go for her source of strength, she used the abilities and resources God had given her and trusted Him for the rest.

The Bible does not tell us when she died or if she even lived to see her children become great. Her legacy lives on because of how wisely she served as a mother, not by her career successes or the tasks she accomplished. Hurrah for motherhood!

Her name is not "in lights," but all of her children's were. All three of her children were instrumental in the ministry and leadership of Israel. She did not have a great title, but left a wonderful testimony, demonstrating Proverbs 22:1. "A good name is rather to be chosen than great riches, and loving favour rather than silver and gold."

As mothers, we have our own mission field right in our homes. Many times Satan tempts us with conflicting emotions of the pride of a profession versus mothering. How do you feel when people ask, "What do you do?" Are you embarrassed to say you are a homemaker? Let's allow Jochebed's life to encourage us as mothers in the training of our children for Christ. Jochebed was a keeper at home. *(Titus 2:5)* "The hand that rocked the cradle literally ruled the world!" What a joy to train our children with the hope of one day seeing them loving and serving God with their own families.

Jochebed's Roles	Jochebed's Character Traits
1. Wife	1. Determination
2. Mother	2. Creativity
3. Nursemaid	3. Poise
4. Servant	4. Self-control
5. Teacher	5. Balance
	6. Courage
	7. Imagination
	8. Resourcefulness

Chapter 5

THE VIRTUOUS WOMAN

"An Excellent Homemaker"

Facts	
Husband:	Unnamed
Children:	Unnamed
Occupation:	Housewife, Mother

Introduction

(Job 28:18; Prov. 8:11; 12:4; 31:1-2, 10)

"Mirror, Mirror on the wall, who's the fairest of them all?"
The virtuous woman! What a role model for us as ladies! What a godly example the Proverbs 31 woman is to us.

Often ladies are intimidated by the study of the virtuous woman and think, "I could never do all of that!" However, just as we will *never* be perfect Christians, so we will never be perfect women. But, shouldn't we strive for the "best?" The Bible paints that best for us in this lady of virtue.

Proverbs 31 is written like a mother or father admonishing a son as we see the words "my son, my son" in the beginning. Some commentators say that King Lemuel wrote it as his mother had instructed him; others say Solomon wrote it as Bathsheba had instructed him and perhaps she called Solomon "Lemuel." Whichever the case, we know it is full of rich nuggets about choosing the right wife. Verses 10-31 are often called the "ABC's of the perfect wife." It is written as a challenge or given as a mirror to us from which to pattern our own lives as women.

Matthew Henry said, "This description of the virtuous woman is designed to show what wives the women should make and what wives the men should choose." So, we see two purposes in these Scriptures: becoming a good wife or choosing a good wife.

The passage begins by confirming that a virtuous woman is difficult to find. The rhetorical question states, "Who can find?" She is difficult to find! We know that to be very true from our society today. Few daughters are trained to be virtuous women. A virtuous woman is a rare treasure; in fact, such a rare treasure that the Bible says her price is "far above rubies." What do we see rubies linked with throughout the Bible? That's right! – wisdom! Wisdom is "above rubies," "better than rubies." *(Job 28:18, Prov. 8:11)* So, we see the virtuous woman linked to wisdom.

The virtuous woman is morally excellent, upright, and chaste. The Hebrew term used for virtuous is *chayil*, meaning "valiant, strong, worthy." A man is fortunate who finds such a woman. Let's look at the other qualities she possesses.

Commitments at Home (Prov. 31:13-22, 24, 27)

The verbs and adverbs in the following passage are emboldened. *(Prov. 31:13-22, 24, 27)*

> She **seeketh** wool, and flax, and **worketh willingly** with her hands.
> She is like the merchant's ships; she **bringeth** her food from afar.
> She **riseth** also while it is yet night, and **giveth** meat to her
>   household, and a portion to her maidens.
> She **considereth** a field, and **buyeth** it: with the fruit of her hands
>   she **planteth** a vineyard.
> She **girdeth** her loins with strength, and **strengtheneth** her arms.
> She **perceiveth** that her merchandise is good: her candle **goeth not
>   out** by night.
> She **layeth** her hands to the spindle, and her hands **hold** the distaff.
> She **stretcheth out** her hand to the poor; yea, she **reacheth forth** her
>   hands to the needy.

Helpmeets & Homemakers
Women of the Bible, volume 1

> She **is not afraid** of the snow for her household: for all her household **are clothed** with scarlet.
> She **maketh** herself coverings of tapestry; her clothing is silk and purple.
> She **maketh** fine linen, and **selleth** it; and **delivereth** girdles unto the merchant.
> She **looketh well** to the ways of her household, and **eateth not** the bread of idleness.

What can we notice about these verbs? The virtuous woman was always in an action mode like the "drive" on a car. We do not ever see her in neutral, park, (idle), or reverse! She had many jobs, showing she was industrious and orderly. Oh, you may say, "Here we go! Neat freak! It's just not my personality!" You know, it should be because the Bible shows us God is a God of order and not the author of confusion. The virtuous woman managed her home and managed it well! She earned money and invested it. It seems she may have had a home business. Let's consider her different jobs.

The first job described is that of working in textiles. Notice she did not wait for someone to give her the material or even ask for it. The Bible says she "seeketh" wool. Then when she had the material, she immediately put it to use by putting her hands to the spindle and distaff. She did not waste time or material! *(Prov. 31:13, 19, 24)*

Her other home jobs were farming and gardening. However, before she could begin this venture, we see her even purchasing the land. She had good business sense and did not buy the first thing she saw. Not being hasty, she *considered* the field and then bought it. After the purchase, the field did not lie fallow. She followed through and planted a vineyard to gain food for her family. *(Prov. 31:16)*

It seems this lady was probably involved in a home business also as we see her making fine linen and selling it. Then she delivered girdles or belts to the merchants also. *(Prov. 31:24)* Using her talents and creativity, she earned extra finance for her home. We see that her jobs were all womanly jobs and connected with the home. Often she worked late into the night to complete her jobs. She took pride in the things she made and sold only the best.

In the midst of all her work, she maintained a willing spirit. She did not fear hard work or expect others to wait on her. Being a capable homemaker, she shopped for food, looked for bargains, and even arose early to cook the food for her family and her maidens. *(Prov. 31:14-15)* What a servant's heart she demonstrated! Mothers not only should demonstrate these traits, but fervently train their daughters in them, also.

We also see her making clothing for her family and using a spindle and a distaff. A spindle is "a rod used in hand spinning to twist into thread the fibers drawn from the distaff." The distaff was a long implement for holding wool. She did not fear the winter as she was prepared for emergencies. Her family had warm clothing and she had enough oil for her candles. *(Prov. 31:18-21)*

What an industrious woman she was! She did not sleep in late or "lay in bed" all morning and let the family members care for themselves! She arose early and stayed up late. Matthew Henry said, "those that have a family to take care of should not love their bed too well in a morning." She was a wise organizer of her time and enjoyed crafts. She made pretty things for her home called tapestries, a woven fabric often used for wall hangings or furniture coverings.

Today we see so many restless women. However, the virtuous woman was not restless and did not consider homemaking a "tie-down," or a yoke. Unlike the women libbers of our age, she loved homemaking and did not feel it was an "abridgement of her liberty." What a godly example to us ladies of today!

Often it is difficult for us as ladies to maintain a willing heart and a cheerful spirit in our duties as wives and mothers. We are constantly cleaning, cooking, and caring only to get up the next day to repeat the routine. However, when we realize the lives we are affecting and how our attitude affects the home, it motivates us to face each new day in a time alone with God for strength for that day. We think, "There is no way I could be like that woman!" None of can on our own, but God can enable us to get the job done. Instead of looking at the whole week's work at once, trust God to help you accomplish one day's tasks at a time or even one hour's. Limit phone calls, TV programs, and coffee breaks and minimize trips to the store. Yes, we all need times to share with friends, but not at the expense of our homes and families. Often we are too restless and continually "on the run."

We see the virtuous woman out of her home mainly to do her chores and business dealings. We do not see her running back and forth to others' homes all day long. How did she get it all done? By taking one day at a time. Perhaps she had a list and checked off each chore as she finished it. Remember she did not do all of these things in one day!

Likewise, you can space your jobs out. Maybe one day could be laundry day, one day sweeping, one day cleaning the bathrooms, etc. Other older godly women can give you advice about your schedules also. Ask God to give you a willing heart and a right attitude about your home commitments.

Care of Husband and Children
(Prov. 12:4; 31:11-12, 23, 27-8)

Not only was the virtuous woman committed to caring for her home, but her family as well. Imagine how the husband of this woman felt! He enjoyed returning to a clean home, well-cared for children, and scrumptious food on the table. How he must have appreciated his wife! Scripture tells us he had full confidence in her and trusted her. What a blessing! He never worried that she would run off with his best friend. Proverbs 31:11 states "The heart of her husband doth safely trust in her, so that he shall have no need of spoil." She did not waste his hard-earned money as it was too difficult to acquire. He trusted in her chastity, her conduct, and her fidelity. Proverbs 12:4 tells us that "a virtuous woman is a crown to her husband." She was his queen and made him feel like a king! She brought honor to her husband and would not damage his reputation. What a super helpmeet! Providing his meals, laundering his clothes, making her home a haven, and loving him were all things she enjoyed doing, not dreaded. Her biblical, godly pattern challenged and fulfilled her. To top it all, she realized this was not just for the good days, but for "all the days of her life." *(Prov. 31:12)* Remember those vows – "till death us do part?" She took her marriage seriously and did not want to make her husband ashamed. He was known in the community and she helped to make it so. *(Prov. 31:23)* Her husband praised and loved her.

Likewise, she was a good mother to her children. She fed and clothed them and knew what was going on in the home. A woman "on the run" cannot look well to the ways of her household. Not so with the virtuous woman! She kept her eye on things and did not leave the children unchaperoned or alone.*(Prov. 29:15)* Training takes time and she gave herself to the task. Because of this, her children would "arise up and call her blessed" also.

Are you caring for your husband and children? Or do they mostly fend for themselves and have to adjust to your schedule? Can your husband trust in you and are you helping him form a good reputation? Does your husband enjoy or dread coming home at the end of each day? Do you take time to train and listen to your children? Remember, God will enable you as He did the virtuous woman.

Care of Self   (Prov. 31:17, 22, 25-27, 29-30; Matt. 12:34)

Though the virtuous woman was a busy homemaker, mother, and wife, she realized she needed to take care of herself also. The Scripture shows us that she took physical care of herself.

This physical care involved girding her loins and strengthening her arms. Perhaps she did exercises like push-ups or sit-ups. We know she was by no means a lazy person and she did get exercise through her gardening also. She had to have good health to keep the schedule she kept. She also knew how to dress and keep herself beautiful and appealing to her husband. She used the best material, silk, and the most beautiful of colors, purple. Being a daughter of the king, she dressed like one and was not drab, shabby, or "dowdy" looking! *(Prov. 31:22)* Remember, others in the community were watching her! She had a name to live up to. "A lazy, slovenly, untidy Christian is as much a dishonor to Christ as one who is vain, haughty, or boastful." *(McAllister)*

Though physical care is important, the virtuous woman also knew she had to maintain emotional control. She had strength, honor, and joy! She was not always worried about what tomorrow would bring! In fact, the Bible uses the words, "Strength and honor are her clothing . . ." She was covered with them!

She possessed great spiritual traits. Tongue control was a great asset to her. She did not run from house to house talking. She could not as she had too many responsibilities, looking well to the ways of her own household. Proverbs 31:26 says "She openeth her mouth with wisdom; and in her tongue is the law of kindness." She had the law of kindness and spoke out of the abundance of her heart. She probably avoided people who always talked about or "put down" others. What gave her such good control? The fear of the Lord! ". . .a woman that feareth the Lord, she shall be praised." *(Prov. 31:30)* We know from Scripture that the fear of the Lord is the beginning of wisdom and now we see how she spoke with wisdom. The fear of the Lord gave her great spirituality.

The virtuous woman was an intelligent lady. She learned how to plant a garden, how to sew, how to cook, how to manage her home. It takes a lot of "know-how" to run a home properly.

Once again we see her willingness to learn and do these things. The passage ends with pointing out that she excelled many others.

Since we belong to the Lord Jesus Christ, we should take care of ourselves. We are His and have been bought with a great price. He now lives within us and we represent Him wherever we go. Do we convey a good physical appearance? Do we possess emotional control? Do we fear the Lord and have a close walk with Him? Are we willing to learn new things that will benefit our families? Can it be said that we "excellest them all?"

Compassion for Others   (Deut. 15:11; Prov. 22:9; 31:20, 26)

This busy woman also took time to think of others. God burdened her heart for the poor and needy. Scripture even states she reached forth *both* hands to the needy. At first she stretched out her hand. She then became so concerned that she reached with both hands. Perhaps she gave food, clothing, or finance to those less fortunate. What an unselfish spirit she demonstrated! God was surely pleased with her tender heart as He commands us in Scripture to open wide our hand unto the poor and needy. She even took care of her maidens, not waiting for them to care for her.

Since she was kind and possessed wisdom, perhaps others went to her for counsel. Maybe she was able to share with them things she had learned in managing her home and caring for her family.

Consecration to God   (Prov. 1:7; 9:10; 31:30-31)

The crowning factor in a virtuous woman's life is her relationship with the Lord. What good does it do you to look beautiful, to be physically fit, or to possess emotional control, when your relationship with Christ has sadly deteriorated? Or perhaps you have never had a relationship with Christ. The Proverbs 31 woman definitely had a walk with God. Her fear of the Lord brought the praise of others. She deserved this praise.

She reaped praise because she built a good reputation; she avoided the appearance of evil; and she was too busy to make provision for the flesh to fulfill the lusts thereof. *(Rom. 13:14)*

Having a balance of inward and outward beauty, she is a prime example of 2 Peter 1:5-8. She added to her faith and continued to strive for the best.

How is your walk with God? Are you sowing good seed? Will your children and husband rise up and call you blessed? How about those in your community?

Can you take this pattern and apply it to your life today or will you be like the man in James 1:23-24 - a hearer, but not a doer? Why not strive for the IDEAL, remembering we will not be perfect? Let's use Proverbs 31 as a springboard to improvement and as a pattern to closely follow in our day.

The V.W.'s Roles

1. Mother
2. Wife
3. Cook
4. Manager
5. Organizer
6. Seamstress
7. Servant
8. Gardener

The V.W.'s Character Traits

1. Kindness
2. Ambition
3. Compassion
4. Faithfulness
5. Willingness
6. Joyfulness
7. Orderliness
8. Wisdom
9. Fear of the Lord

NOTES:

Chapter 6

MARY

The Perfect Picture of Submission

Facts	
Husband:	Joseph
Children:	Jesus, James, Joses, Simon, Judas, Unnamed daughters
Occupation:	Housewife
Her name means:	"bitterness," "exalted"

Her Early Life

(Matt. 1:16, 18-19; Luke 1:26-27; 3:23)

Mary was a humble peasant girl who lived in a small village called Nazareth, generally known for its "lack of culture and rude dialect." *(New Ungers, p. 907)* She was from the tribe of Judah and the line of David, royal seed. Tradition says her parents' names may have been Jehoiachim and Anna. Her own name is a form of Marah and Miriam. Scripture reveals nothing of her home life.

However, in Luke 1:27, we do find she was espoused to Joseph, the son of Heli. Another word for espoused is betrothed which means "to be promised in marriage," *(Vine's, N.T. Section, p. 64)* similar to our engagement period of today. The betrothal was a "formal proceeding." Vows or oaths confirmed the ceremony and presents were given to the bride. A feast topped off the celebration and modern Jews even gave "their intended" a ring that signified a "token of fidelity and of adoption into a family." *(New Ungers, p. 818)* Jewish betrothal could be broken only by a divorce and usually lasted a period of one year with no physical relationship taking place.

We see from the Scriptures that Mary was a virgin, clean and pure and that Joseph was a just man. Little did this couple know what was soon to cloud their relationship and what decisions they would face! They were to be mighty instruments used for the glory of God.

Her Supernatural Visit   (Isa. 7:14-16; Micah 5:2; Luke 1:26-38)

Perhaps Mary was going about her daily chores or routine when the angel Gabriel appeared to her. We see from the angel's words what God thought about this young, poor, peasant girl. He called her highly favored and blessed **among** women. Notice he did not say blessed **above** women. McGee says, "She is not lifted above women; she lifted womanhood." A woman was the instrument that brought sin into the world, but God used a woman to bring a Saviour into the world also.

Imagine Mary's surprise by the angel's visit! Luke 1:29 says she was troubled at his saying and wondered what he meant by his salutation. She must have been fearful as Gabriel told her not to fear because she had found favor with God.

We can also have favor with God. It does not mean anything to Him if we are rich or poor, intelligent or illiterate, renown or unknown. God will use the one who is tender, obedient and submissive to Him, the one who yields his all.

Gabriel proceeded to tell Mary what the Lord's plans were for her. She was going to have a baby boy! Can you see her wondering how this could be? She was even given instructions on naming the child and was told to call him "Jesus." The angel informed her that the Holy Ghost would come upon her and God's power would overshadow her. This child would be the Son of God! Mary's emotions must have been in turmoil. God, in His grace and mercy, gave her someone to share the news with as

Gabriel told her that her barren cousin, Elizabeth, had also conceived a son. This was another proof of God's power due to Elizabeth's age and barrenness.

Why did God choose Mary? She was submissive and obedient, gentle and lowly, and she was spiritually fit. God would not use an unclean vessel. We see Mary as humble with a quiet spirit and self-control. She had probably read the Old Testament prophecies. Had she hoped and prayed to be used of God?

Are we spiritually fit for God to use us? Do we stay in the Word on a daily basis to even know what His will might be for our lives? Do we even **want** to be used by God? Or do we kick and rebel when He reveals His will to us through the Word? Remember, God delights to use a clean vessel.

Her Reaction (Luke 1:29-45)

How did Mary react? Did she kick and rebel at God's will for her life? Did she want her rights and say, "Hey, Lord, this is my body, and I will not be brought to public shame? I'll just run out and get an abortion."

No, we see Mary with a submissive and an obedient spirit in Luke 1:38. She said, "be it unto me according to thy word." Even though she was troubled, she did not argue or question, but kept the thoughts in her mind displaying great self-control. It was natural for her to fear. McGee says "when the supernatural touches the natural, it creates fear." We are to fear a holy God. She asked only the one question, "How shall this be seeing I know not a man?" *(Luke 1:34)* Mary faced some tough days ahead. She would be looked upon as a harlot. Embarrassment would pervade her life. "That which conferred upon her the highest honor…would…bring upon her the greatest possible dishonor." *(Spurgeon)*

She traveled to see her friend, her cousin Elizabeth, with whom she would stay for three months. God gave her a like-minded, godly friend with whom to share the news, someone who was herself going through a supernatural experience.

Elizabeth lived in Judah and one scholar speculates that Mary's conception may have taken place there. *(Luke 1:45)* This would have been fitting as:

1. The seed of David was in Judah.
2. Circumcision began there with the promise of Isaac.
3. Old Testament couples are buried there.

Her older friend and relative, encouraging her and building her up was a good example of Titus 2:3-5 of the aged women teaching the younger. Elizabeth called her blessed among women and said she was blessed because she believed. She did not express doubts or fears to discourage the younger woman, but told her there would "be a performance of those things which were told her from the Lord." *(Luke 1:45)*

Do we encourage our friends like Elisabeth did? Do we encourage new converts? Are they able to come and share with us? If we are saved, we have already had a supernatural experience. Can we rejoice in their supernatural experience too? Do we encourage and edify a friend when she is struggling with God's will for her life? Or, do we become negative and say, "I do not know how it is going to work out for you, either." What a good example Elizabeth is to us!

Her Song (Luke 1:46-56)

After the encouragement from Elizabeth, Mary's heart was filled with such joy that she burst forth with a song. This song, known as the "Magnificat," is considered a choice piece of Hebrew literature. Much of this song came from Hannah's song in 1 Samuel 2. She quoted from fifteen Old Testament sources in her song, showing us her knowledge of the Scriptures.

She praised the Lord throughout her song for His attributes: grace, power, mercy, holiness, goodness, faithfulness. Her song shows her reverence and her own personal devotion as she used the words, "my spirit," and "my soul." Mary even knew that she needed a Saviour as expressed in her words, "And my spirit hath rejoiced in God **my** Saviour." *(Luke 1:47)* We see her humility expressed in Luke 1:48 as she realized God was the One Who had regarded her low estate and was blessing her with this great privilege.

She demonstrated her belief that God would scatter the proud, bring down rulers, exalt the lowly, fill the hungry and send the rich away empty. She served a just God and knew He would show mercy! *(Luke 1:51-54)*

Joseph's Reaction (Deut. 22:22-24; Matt. 1:19-25)

We do not know how Joseph discovered the situation about Mary. Did she meet with him and tell him about the angel, Gabriel? Imagine his heartache and dismay when he heard of the pregnancy! Did it shake his faith in his beloved Mary? With his kind, compassionate, and gentle spirit, he thought he would "put her away privily." The least attention to the matter the better! A "public example" could have meant some form of punishment as the law stated that a betrothed virgin who had committed immorality should be stoned." *(Deut. 22:23-24)* Joseph did not make a rash or quick decision. He mulled it over and pondered it. Perhaps he prayed over the situation also.

As Joseph thought the matter over, God in His perfect timing sent an angel to him in a dream. The angel told Joseph not to be afraid because this was a supernatural occurrence. Joseph received instructions to name the child, "Jesus." Joseph obeyed immediately and took Mary for his wife! What better earthly parents could Jesus have had than those who feared and obeyed God? Joseph was chosen of God specifically for this time.

Notice that God spoke to both Joseph and Mary individually. Often, as wives, we want our husbands to change in some area. So we will nag, beg, plead, connive, etc. to try to bring about that change. If we would just take our desires to the Lord! Perhaps during those three months at Elizabeth's house, Mary specifically sought God about the situation with Joseph. How would she ever make him understand this bittersweet situation? How about if she did not tell him and they just got married? As she left the timing up to God, God came on the scene and gave Joseph specific guidance about how to handle the problem.

Psalm 62:5 says, "My soul, wait thou **only** upon God; for my expectation is from him." Can we give our expectations for our husbands over to the Lord? We want them to be the spiritual leaders of our homes, but begging, coercing, and nagging will not convince them. The Lord **can** convince them through His Word and the convicting power of the Holy Spirit.

Let's be patient like Mary and watch what God will do in our husband's lives.

Her Motherhood <small>(Psa. 69:8; Matt. 2:13-14, 22-23; 13:55-56; Mark 6:3; Luke 2:1-7, 22-24, 40-41, 52; John 2:1; 19:25; Acts 1:14)</small>

God's plan even included the time and place that the babe would be born. A tax law was issued and Joseph and Mary had to travel to Bethlehem to pay their taxes. Mary was in her last trimester of pregnancy, probably the last month. What a trip this would be for her! Their destination was approximately seventy miles away, a hop, skip, and jump for us today. However, for Joseph and Mary, this would take several days. Mary was in a strange place with no midwife, no doctor, or hospital. God had handpicked Bethlehem. Bethlehem means "house of bread." How fitting for the Bread of Life to be born there.

We do not see Mary complaining about her circumstances. She "rolled with the punches" so to speak. Though there was no room in the inn, God provided a stable for the birth of His special son. She did not have her mother to stay with her to help prepare meals or to give guidance on baby care. She leaned totally on the Lord and the advice of her husband.

After circumcising Jesus on the eighth day and following her days of purification, Mary and Joseph took their babe to Jerusalem to present Him to the Lord. Their sacrifice of turtledoves shows the poverty of their home. We see from the beginning how they were faithful to keep their child in church and obey the things they knew to obey.

Mary moved three times. The first move was from Nazareth to Bethlehem where Jesus was born. Then the family moved from Bethlehem to Egypt after Joseph was warned in a dream that King Herod sought to kill the child. It was ironic that God would choose Egypt as a haven for the child. Mary was constantly on the move in the early years of her marriage. From Egypt the family then moved back to Nazareth after being instructed by an angel that Herod was dead. However, when Joseph heard that Herod's son reigned in his place, he chose Nazareth for their permanent home. God totally guided this young family! We see Mary willingly following wherever her godly husband led.

We know that Mary mothered Christ for 30 years though He was out in His public ministry and not often home. The Bible tells us she had other children. We know she had to have at least seven including Jesus, as Matthew 13:55 lists four brothers names, and the next verse lists sisters as plural.

Mary was a busy mother and housewife. She trained Jesus as Luke 2:52 verifies that He grew in wisdom. She also kept Him in church, as they were faithful to go every year to the Passover. Do our children see us busy for the Lord? Are we faithful to the church services or do we let any little flimsy excuse keep us at home? Are we taking time to train our little ones in godly character traits or are we too busy pursuing our own interests and friends that our children are neglected? What an example Mary is to us as a helpmeet and a homemaker!

Though Mary stayed busy as a wife and a mother, she still had time for some social events. In John 2:1 we find her attending a wedding. We know she had other lady friends as she was found at the cross with her sister, another Mary, and Mary Magdalene.

As mentioned previously, she was found in church at the appointed times. What better people are there to socialize with than other like-minded believers? Are you neglecting this important area of your life? Do you look forward to the worship services and activities that your church has to offer? We need to forsake not the assembling of ourselves together. *(Heb. 10:25)*

Last but not least, we find Mary at a prayer meeting in Acts 1:14. It appears that she knew how to intercede and seek God for others. Mary had a walk with God.

Her Suffering

(Matt. 12:46-50; Mark 3:31; Luke 2:34-35, 42-51; John 2:1-5; 19:25-27)

Mary knew she would suffer in this life. Simeon had prophesied of it when they dedicated Jesus and told her a sword would someday pierce her own soul. Though she was the mother of Jesus, "Mary was to experience darkness as well as delight." *(Lockyer, p. 96)* Because Mary had a close walk with God and sweet communion with Him, she withstood the sufferings that came her way. We never know the trials or troubles that will come into our lives. It is imperative that we maintain a close relationship with our Saviour so when the trials beset us, we will be fortified through the Word we have learned.

We find Mary's first trial early in her life. She was filled with public shame and humiliation. Imagine the disgust and reproach she faced because of the pregnancy out of wedlock. The situation even brought danger her way, as the consequence for such a sin was death! God proved faithful to her throughout this time.

Her second trial caused much fear and anxiety as her own government threatened her child's life and the family had to seek exile in Egypt. Once again, God proved faithful to them and warned them giving them time to escape.

In Luke 2:42-45 we find another trial in the young couple's life. They were traveling to Jerusalem for the Passover and lost their twelve year-old son, Jesus! Imagine how they felt! He was missing from their loving care for four days as they traveled a day's journey before they were even aware of it. They returned to Jerusalem and searched for him for three days! Mary's heart was probably broken. Did she blame herself for not keeping a closer eye on Him? Perhaps they thought He was with relatives and was just socializing. Upon finding Him, Mary was the first to speak and asked Him why He had done such a thing? She admitted she and Joseph had agonized over his disappearance. " . . .behold thy father and I have sought thee sorrowing." *(Luke 2:48)* They did not understand Jesus' answer to them about doing His Father's business. "Her 'lost boy' was to be God's only hope for a 'lost world.' " *(Lockyer, p. 96)*

It is a tragic event to lose a child as a parent's mind always jumps to the things that could have happened to Him. Mary was probably seeking God for those few days and asking Him to help them find her son.

Mary's next trial could have been an early widowhood, as Joseph is not mentioned again after this incident with Jesus in the temple. In Mark 3:31, the Scripture says "his brethren and his mother" were looking for Him. At the wedding in Cana of Galilee, the Scripture says "the mother of Jesus was there . . ." Nothing is said of Joseph. If Mary faced an early widowhood, she had to trust the Lord for provision and guidance. Perhaps she was familiar with Isaiah 54:5 which says "for thy maker is thine husband . . ." She had seen God intervene in the protection of Jesus throughout His baby days. Now she just had to take God at His Word that He would take care of her. After all, if Joseph died when Jesus was a teenager, she had to finish raising at least seven children without their father. This was no easy task! She must have been a very hard-working and godly woman.

It is ironic that a later trial took place at a gala event. It was a happy and exciting time for Mary as Jesus was beginning His earthly ministry! It would be great to witness a miracle at a wedding! She approached Jesus and told Him there was no wine. There are different thoughts about what this meant. Mary must have been a close friend or relative of the wedding party and may have been part of those who served. Some think the family was poor and ran out of refreshments. Perhaps Mary felt badly for her friends and was trying to avert their embarrassment. Others say this was a gentle hint for Jesus and His disciples to leave since there was no food left. (Isn't that just like a mom? Still teaching manners?) Still others think Mary was suggesting that Jesus give a little speech. Did she perhaps want a miracle to clear her own name and reputation? However, this was Jesus' first miracle, so she was not even aware that He could perform miracles. Mary was probably leaning on her thirty year-old son to solve the problem. Joseph apparently was not present and she was looking to her oldest son for help in the situation. Perhaps she had leaned on Him before in time of trouble. Maybe He could arrange with someone to get some more, or in some way manage the situation.

When Jesus responded to Mary's statement, He called her "woman" instead of mother. This was not showing disrespect but a tender address that Christ also later used from the Cross. Mary could not control what God would do through Jesus. He was no longer a child, but a man! Their relationship was beginning to change, kind of like sending your child off to college. After this, Scripture does not show him returning at any time to His earthly home again. This event probably hurt Mary's soft heart.

It is hard to let go of our children. We need to be willing to let God use our children no matter what. He may call them to some type of full time Christian work. Will we encourage them or discourage them? Will we just look on the material side of the issue and tell them how much better a different type of job would pay? Aren't there eternal rewards and the importance of winning souls for Christ to consider?

Jesus pointed to His Sonship when Mary and the family approached Him in Matthew 12. Their relationship had changed. He asked who His mother and His brethren were. He then proceeded to say that anyone who does the will of the Father is his brother, sister, and mother. Those who serve must leave all. Having to say good-bye to your family and not knowing when or if you will see them again must be the most difficult obstacle of serving on a mission field. Jesus knew the exact feelings of leaving His Heavenly Father to come to His earthly mission field.

Mary's final and deepest suffering was seeing the child, whom she had brought into the world, die a horrible cruel death on the cross. Though their relationship had changed, we still see Christ's compassion for His earthly mother here. He entrusted her care and oversight to His disciple, John, thereby ensuring her provision. This seems to verify her widowhood. Matthew Henry said, "Sometimes when God removes one comfort from us, He raises up another for us." John 19:27 tells us that from that hour, John "took her unto his own home." One can only imagine the sorrow and bitterness Mary experienced over seeing her firstborn so tortured and mistreated! Only the comfort of the Holy Spirit could sustain her through such a terrible ordeal. Her mother's heart probably wanted to lash out at the injustice of it all! She may have faced sleepless nights and depression. Jesus knew she would need John's home to be a haven to her.

Perhaps as a mother, your heart is hurting today over some trial with your child or children. You may have a wayward child or a child with a dreaded disease. Maybe you are drinking a cup of suffering like Mary did. The comfort of the Holy Spirit will sustain and keep you through it. The Bible says, " . . .weeping may endure for a night, but joy cometh in the morning." *(Psa. 30:5b)* There will be an end to your trial! Psalm 57:1b verifies this by promising, " . . .in the shadow of thy wings will I make my refuge, **until these calamities be overpast.**" Little did Mary know the joy she was to experience in a few days when her son would miraculously be resurrected from the grave! Rest in the shadow of His wings!

Her Privileges and Sacrifices

Mary and Joseph may have lived with a shameful reputation of Christ's birth. Perhaps the Pharisees were taunting Jesus in John 8:19 when they asked him "Where is thy Father?" To many, Jesus looked like an illegitimate child.

Though they experienced privileges from parenting Jesus, there were also sacrifices to make. Mary learned that "exceptional privilege often goes hand in hand with sacrifice." *(Karssen, Book 1, p. 132)* What were some of these sacrifices and privileges that Mary and Joseph made?

Privileges	Sacrifices
1. Availability to God	1. Loss of reputation
2. Earthly parents of Christ	2. Loss of physical union until His birth
3. Naming the child	3. Loss of their own good name
4. Educating the child	4. Loss of Son at early age
5. Home/friends for child	5. Loss of their own friends

Conclusions

Mary continued to serve God in spite of personal loss. Though she lived under a cloud her whole life, she did not let it affect her spiritually. She kept a song in her heart and a smile on her lips. There are different clouds we may face: clouds of grief, clouds of bad disease, clouds of broken relationships, clouds of financial problems, etc. We must not allow those clouds to hinder our walk with our Lord and Saviour. Can we follow Mary's example and remain faithful during those times?

Mary, the first lady of the New Testament, is in direct contrast with Eve, the first lady of the Old Testament. Eve ignored God's will whereas Mary chose to follow God's will. Eve chose her own will, comfort, and convenience. Mary chose to embrace God's will despite public opinion and the scars it would leave. Eve brought sin into the world, but Mary brought the Saviour into the world. Eve found bitterness and sorrow, but Mary found blessing and joy.

False Teachings Regarding Mary

The Roman Catholic religion teaches at least five false things concerning Mary:

1. **Immaculate Conception** – They say that Mary was not cursed by original sin and never sinned later in life. This sets her apart from the rest of the human race. They say that even her own conception was a miracle! This thought was established in the twelfth century and became a papal decree in 1854. There is absolutely no Scripture to bear this out as we see that Mary even recognized her own need for a Saviour in her Magnificat. *(Luke 1:47)*

2. **"Assumptio Mariae"** – or Mary's Ascension. They teach that Mary died, rose again, and ascended to Heaven. No one knows where she was buried, right? This teaching started in 1950.

3. **Perpetual virginity** – Taking Scripture totally out of context in Ezekiel 44:2, the Catholics teach that Mary remained a virgin and never had any other children after Christ. They totally ignore Matthew 12:46, 13:55, or Mark 6:3 where it talks about His brothers and His sisters.

4. **Mary as mediator** – According to the Catholic faith, Mary "represents the infinite love and mercy of God for the sinner." "It is not Jesus but Mary who saves the sinner!" *(Chiniquy, p. 38)* 'From the church he (the baptized Roman Catholic) learns the example of holiness and recognizes its model and source in the all-holy virgin Mary.' *(Bennett, p. 361)*

However, 1 Timothy 2:5 tells us "For there is one God, and one mediator between God and men, the **man Jesus Christ**." Likewise Hebrews 9:11-12 says, "But Christ being come an high priest of good things to come, by a greater and more perfect tabernacle, not made with hands, that is to say, not of this building; Neither by the blood of goats and calves, but by his own blood he entered in once into the holy place, having obtained eternal redemption for us."

5. **Mary the Mother of God**

The idea here is that as Christ's mother, she can tell Him what to do or at least He will do whatever she wants. There have even been serious attempts to make the Trinity a foursome by deifying Mary.

None of these teachings on Mary bare any Scriptural evidence. They are man-made teachings and rituals. The Catholic religion is taken up with Mariolatry – the excessive "ritual act of devotion" to Mary.

'Mariolatry belongs, historically, to unauthorized speculation; and psychologically, to the natural history of asceticism and clerical celibacy . . .' Rome's exaltation of Mary consists largely of fictitious and unreliable legends and dogmas. The true Christian portrayal of the mother of Jesus is that to be found only in the gospels in which the Master taught that man has access to God only through **His** all-sufficient mediatorial work. *(Lockyer, p. 99)*

Helpmeets & Homemakers
Women of the Bible, volume 1

Mary was just a woman like you or me—a woman who knew she needed a Saviour, a woman who loved and obeyed God, a woman who served God. She is a wonderful pattern to us of a good wife and mother, but she should not be worshipped.

The last mention of Mary in the Bible is at a prayer meeting. In spite of her personal loss and grief, she remained faithful to the Lord and the early fellowship of believers. What a lasting impression of her that God has left for us!

Mary's Roles

1. Wife
2. Mother
3. Songwriter
4. Widow

Mary's Character Traits

1. Obedience
2. Humility
3. Faithfulness
4. Unselfishness
5. Gratefulness
6. Ambition
7. Piety

NOTES:

Chapter 7

ELISABETH
The "Sarah" of the New Testament

Facts	
Husband:	Zacharias
Children:	John the Baptist
Occupation:	Housewife, Mother, Preacher's wife
Her name means:	"God is my oath," "a worshipper of God"

The Family's Background (1 Chr. 24:5, 10, 18- 19; Luke 1:5-7)

Elisabeth was a preacher's wife and was married to Zacharias, a priest of the order of Abia. Priests were divided into twenty-four groups with each group serving two weeks per year. This opportunity came by drawing lots as explained in 1 Chronicles 24:5, 18-19. It appears that Elisabeth, herself, had perhaps been a preacher's daughter as Scripture tells us she was from the daughters of Aaron. *(Luke 1:5)*

The Bible shares with us three of this godly couple's character traits in Luke 1:6. It specifically states that "they were **both** righteous," obedient, and blameless! What a testimony they upheld. Could that be said of you?

Nothing is told of Elisabeth's younger years. As the story opens, we find this older couple with no children. In fact, the Bible says "they both were now well stricken in years." *(Luke 1:7)* Though they were godly, they had never been blessed with children. Imagine their disappointment! Though we live godly, everything will not be perfect in our lives. Had Elisabeth and

Zacharias become bitter and given up on God? No, indeed! They were still at their posts of worship and service!

Remember the heartache of barrenness? It was a disgrace not to have any children. People usually thought there was sin in the life of the parents. Not only did these dear people suffer the heartache of having no children, but they were perhaps scorned and ridiculed also.

The Angel's Visit   (Luke 1:8-17, 28-29)

Once again we see someone just going about his daily routine when the Lord intervenes. Zacharias was being faithful to his Lord and his job. "A routine event became part of a divine plan." His job was to burn incense in the temple. Some say it was a one-time event as there were so many priests. As Zacharias was going about his duty, an angel appeared to him, troubling him and causing him much fear! *(Luke 1:12)* Remember Mary's response? She likewise was troubled when an angel appeared to her also. *(Luke 1:28-29)*

Zacharias must have been seeking the Lord about his wife's barrenness as in Luke 1:13 the angel told him to fear not and that his prayer was heard. Matthew Henry said, "Prayers of faith are filed in Heaven and are not forgotten though the thing prayed for is not presently given." This is the only instance in the Bible where we read of an angel from God appearing in the temple with a message.

What was that message? Gabriel told Zacharias that his wife would have a son and just as with Mary and Joseph, Zacharias was given specific instructions on what to name the child. The child was to be named John. The angel also predicted much joy and gladness with many rejoicing over the upcoming birth.

Continuing with his message, Gabriel said the child would be great and filled with the Holy Ghost. He was going to be a pure vessel and was not to drink wine or strong drink. John's main goal would be to point people to Christ. He would be the forerunner of Christ and a great soulwinner. What qualifications for service he would possess!

Zacharias' Response (Dan. 8:16, 9:21; Luke 1:18-23, 62)

Zacharias could not believe his ears! "You've got to be kidding!" How could this be? I am too old! Isn't that just like us today? We pray and pray for something and when God answers that prayer, we are dumbfounded. Because God's ways are not our ways, we often think His answer cannot be the right one and we have doubtful thoughts just like Zacharias.

The angel introduced himself as Gabriel and told Zacharias that God had sent him to give the message. By introducing himself, Gabriel demonstrated his authority. Gabriel had also been sent to Daniel in the Old Testament to tell of the Messiah's coming. *(Dan. 8:16, 9:21)* Gabriel always seems to be linked with the Messiah and announcing someone coming.

Because of his doubt and disbelief, Zacharias was chastised and lost his speech and his hearing until the child was born. *(Luke 1:20, 62)* Unable to boast of the vision or divulge it easily to others, he had to speak using signs and gestures. "His unbelief was silenced and he was silenced for it." *(Matthew Henry)* The people standing outside the temple realized something special had happened to him, as he remained speechless and beckoned to them. Although he was chastised, he finished his job in the temple before returning home. What an example he is to us of maintaining a right spirit toward the Lord during chastening. He did not quit or blame others! He continued serving.

Sometimes we become downhearted and discouraged when the Lord has to chastise us. We skip out of church services and allow our burden for others to dim. We think we deserve better treatment. After all, we are serving the Lord, right? Zacharias did not fall into this trap. He continued in his service for the Lord and Elisabeth stood by him.

Elisabeth's Miracle (Judges 13:14; Luke 1:24-25)

Had Elisabeth been seeking the Lord for a child or had she given up the thought due to her age? Scripture does not reveal this to us. However, Zacharias' prayer was answered and the angel's prophecy was immediately fulfilled as Elisabeth conceived.

She then hid herself for five months. Why did she do this? We can only speculate. She possibly wanted to stay ceremonially clean and pure like Samson's mother in Judges 13:14. Perhaps she wanted to protect the child and did not want to miscarry. Maybe she was ashamed to be that old and pregnant. Was she humble and not desirous to boast of God's honor upon her? Or did she just want time for prayer and praise? Whatever her reason, she did realize this miracle was from the Lord and that her reproach had been removed!

Mary's Visit (Luke 1:36, 39-45)

In the sixth month of her pregnancy, her cousin Mary paid her a visit. As Mary greeted her, the baby leaped in her womb, fulfilling Gabriel's promise in Luke 1:15 that the babe would be "filled with the Holy Ghost, even from his mother's womb." Could this have been a signal to her that the Messiah was at hand? Elisabeth, herself, was filled with the Holy Ghost and began to prophesy with a loud voice. God used her to encourage Mary.

Elisabeth also realized her own need of a Saviour as she said in Luke 1:43, "And whence is this to me, that the mother of **my Lord** should come to me?" The baby's leaping in her womb was a sign to her and she proceeded to reassure Mary that God was going to perform those things He had told her!

What a great visit they must have had as Mary stayed for three months! They had a common bond. Their relationship shows us how much God cares for women and their feelings! He knows we need friendships with other women. He knows our hearts need encouraged from time to time with good Christian fellowship. Notice that these ladies were sharing **good** reports and praises to God, not gossip or negative things! It was a time of rejoicing! Elisabeth truly had gifts of encouragement and edification. What an example she is to us of the aged women described in Titus 2.

John's Birth   (Luke 1:57-68)

When Elisabeth's time came, she delivered a son. Everyone rejoiced just as Gabriel had prophesied. God had once again demonstrated His great mercy. God takes notice. God cares. We see womanhood being exalted here!

After the eighth day, Zacharias and Elisabeth took their infant to be circumcised. They were obedient to God's commands and precepts. Family and friends thought the child should be named after his daddy and tried to force this tradition upon them. Evidently Zacharias had shared the angel's instructions with Elisabeth, as we see her telling the family no. The child would be named John. This caused much conflict as no one in the family had ever heard this name before. They all appealed to Zacharias who wrote, "His name is John." *(Luke 1:63)* Immediately Zacharias' speech problem was resolved and he praised God aloud bringing fear upon all! "Infidelity closed his mouth, and now believing opened it again." *(Matthew Henry)* God rewarded his obedience!

Are we able to stand up to family pressure concerning spiritual things? Elisabeth did not even hesitate or seek other advice. She already had the mind of God on the matter from her godly husband and took her stand. Family pressures can be very intense and make us waver at times. Taking a stand **will** cause conflict. It is a battle we must win. Also, our children need to see us take a stand. When company "drops in" at church time, do we stay home with the company or do we "forsake not the assembling?" Are our standards the same at church **and** at home? As in Elisabeth's case, family will often not understand the stands we do take. However, Paul wrote to the Galatians, "For do I now persuade men, or God? or do I seek to please men? for if I yet pleased men, I should not be the servant of Christ." *(Gal. 1:10)* Servants were even instructed by Paul to obey their masters in all things, "not with eyeservice, as menpleasers; but in singleness of heart, fearing God." *(Col. 3:22)* Elisabeth and Zacharias demonstrated that singleness of heart in the naming of their baby.

Following the naming of the baby, Zacharias was also filled with the Holy Ghost and prophesied of the Redeemer. John was raised in a godly home with Spirit-filled parents.

We hear no more of Elisabeth after this. We do not even know if she had any other children. Her days must have been filled with much joy in the raising of her son for the Lord.

Conclusions   (Matt. 11:11; Luke 1:80; John 3:30)

John grew and "waxed strong in spirit." Oh that our children would wax strong in spirit! Are they waxing strong in other things like sports, ballet, karate, gymnastics, or computer games, but neglecting spiritual things? Where is the emphasis in our homes today? Are we teaching and training our children to be spiritually discerning, to live close to the Lord, and to desire spiritual things? Or, do we have our priorities based on the temporal things of this world?

In Matthew 11:11, Christ complimented Elisabeth when He said, "Among them that are born of women there hath not risen a greater than John the Baptist . . ." She was the "first woman to confess Jesus in the flesh." Being a strong woman of God, she did not "cave in" to the pressures of her day. We do not see any jealousy demonstrated toward Mary. She could have said, "I'm the older woman." "Why can't I have the greater honor?" Perhaps her son John bore her same spirit toward Christ when he said, "He must increase, but I must decrease." *(John 3:30)*

What kind of spirit do our children (and others) witness in our lives? Are we negative and critical most of the time? Do we complain when others are promoted and honored and we are not? Are we willing to "take the back seat" in order to make someone else successful? - to decrease that someone might increase? What valuable lessons John must have learned from His godly parents!

Due to her age at John's birth, Elisabeth may not have lived to witness his horrible death. Perhaps God in His mercy spared her that traumatic event.

Elisabeth demonstrated loyalty to her husband and stood behind him. Though it appears that she had more faith, she did not put him down or try to change him. She loved him for who he was, and allowed God to work on him. She gave her expectations to the Lord. *(Psa. 62:5)* How is it with you? Are you always trying to change your husband or remake him? Do you nag him or belittle him in front of others? This only serves to harden a man's heart. Can you turn those expectations over to the Lord as Psalm 62:5 states?

What an honor Elisabeth experienced in her life! John the Baptist's birth helped pave the way for the virgin birth of Christ. Once again, God used a godly woman to fulfill His plan. Are you willing to be a godly woman so that God can use you in some great way?

Elisabeth's Roles

1. Wife
2. Mother
3. Prophetess
4. Encourager

Elisabeth's Character Traits

1. Faithfulness
2. Unselfishness
3. Determination
4. Humility
5. Loyalty
6. Obedience

NOTES:

Chapter 8

LOIS and EUNICE
"Unfeigned Faith"

Facts – Lois

Husband:	Name unknown
Children:	Eunice
Occupation:	Housewife
Her name means:	"agreeable," "desirable"

Facts - Eunice

Husband:	Greek unnamed
Children:	Timothy
Occupation:	Housewife
Her name means:	"conquering well"

We find one of the shortest biographies ever written in 2 Timothy 1:5. The author is the Holy Spirit; the writer is Paul; and the main characters are Lois, Eunice, and Timothy. Though Lois and Eunice are mentioned by name only once in the entire Bible and that verse appears inconspicuous, their lives impacted the Apostle Paul's ministry and gave the world a pastor in Timothy. Even though their biography is short, it is powerful and should influence us as wives, mothers, and grandmothers of today.

Their Background   (Acts 16:1-3; 2 Tim. 1:5)

Lois and Eunice were a mother-daughter team who lived in Lystra, located in the Roman province of Galatia, also known today as Turkey. Lois was the matriarch of the family and taught her daughter and grandson the Scriptures. Though they knew the Scriptures, they did not know the way of salvation until they heard the Apostle Paul preach on his first missionary journey to Lystra. It appears that this whole family - mother, daughter, and grandson - were converted at that time.

The Bible only uses the word "grandmother" one time and it is in relation to Lois, this godly matriarch.

Lois' daughter, Eunice, had married an unbeliever, a Greek Gentile. From this unequal yoke came the son, Timothy, whose name means "he that fears God." Because of that meaning and the fact that his father was an unbeliever, it is reasonable to assume that his mother probably named him.

Their Influence   (Acts 16:1-3; 2 Tim. 1:5; 3:14-15)

Though Eunice was unable to have the babe circumcised due to her husband's unbelief, she did not let this thwart or prohibit her from teaching her child the Scriptures. Paul affirms this by saying that Timothy had known the Scriptures "from a child." She and grandma Lois were faithful to instruct the child in the Old Testament Bible stories and principles. Did they know the great effect this would have on the little boy? Perhaps they remembered the Scripture in Proverbs 22:6 about training up a child in the way he should go. In any event, they were faithful to their cause as evidenced by Paul when he commended them for their unfeigned faith. The Greek word for unfeigned means "sincere, without hypocrisy." *(Zodhiates)* What a testimony they had! They lived what they taught!

Some authors believe Eunice may have become widowed at an early age and was compelled to work outside the home, though there is no scriptural evidence. Since she and Lois' names are so intertwined in the training, they think grandma may have had

Timothy more in her care than usual. How she must have loved holding the young boy on her lap and singing and reading to him!

It is imperative to begin early in the instruction of our children. Their minds are tender and their hearts are open during the formative years! They are little imitators of everything we do and say. What an opportunity we have as mothers and grandmothers!

As Timothy grew up, his good reputation spread throughout Lystra and Iconium. It appears that Eunice was able to override the ungodly influence of the father with her faithfulness and persistence in training Timothy. Although this does not always happen, "one godly parent may counteract the bad influence of the ungodly and win the child to Christ." *(Lockyer)* She probably knew the Scripture in Proverbs 22:1: "A good name is rather to be chosen than great riches, and loving favour rather than silver and gold." She involved Lois in his care, realizing that "a child left to himself bringeth his mother to shame." *(Prov. 29:15b)*

These scriptural principles still stand for today. We need to teach our children how important a good name is. As Christians, we represent the Lord Jesus Christ. Do we pay our bills? Do we arrive on time? Are we dependable? Are we honest? Do we work hard? Are we faithful to a local Church? Our children see and know our reputation. How can we teach them these things if we do not do them ourselves?

Leaving children to themselves only lays the groundwork for trouble. They may be tempted to do evil things and yield to that temptation just because there is no supervision. We must not give them unsupervised time talking on the telephone, watching TV, or playing computer games. We dare not allow these things become our babysitters, instead of providing other reliable, godly people to supervise them in any absence.

Paul's Influence (Acts 16:1-3; 2 Tim. 1:5; 3:14-15)

Paul dearly loved Timothy and realized his potential. Recognizing his good reputation and his faith, he took Timothy with him on his second missionary journey after circumcising him for the sake of the Jews. Timothy and Silas filled the void for Paul when Paul and Barnabas split up. "Though Paul had lost a brother in Barnabas, he had gained a son in Timothy." *(Deen)*

Years later, Paul trusted Timothy so much that he left him in charge of the church at Ephesus and wrote 1 and 2 Timothy to guide him in his pastoral responsibilities. He looked at Timothy as his son and wrote in his salutation in 1 Timothy, "Unto Timothy, my **own son** in the faith." *(1 Tim. 1:2)* He challenged Timothy to preach the word and warned him against false doctrines. He encouraged Timothy to be faithful and to have courage.

Paul begged Timothy to continue in the things he had learned and been assured of, reminding him that he had known these things from the Scriptures as a child. *(2 Tim. 3:14-15)* What a testimony to Lois and Eunice's training! Paul upheld that testimony before Timothy.

Perhaps Paul filled the role of the godly father Timothy never had. At any rate, there was a great bond between the two as Paul even sought Timothy's comfort and fellowship when he was in prison in Rome. *(2 Tim. 4:9)*

Results of the Training

In the training of her son, Eunice lived up to the meaning of her name, "conquered well." She left a spiritual legacy that would impact the world for centuries to come. Matthew Henry said, "It is a comfortable thing when children imitate the faith and holiness of their godly parents and tread in their steps." Though grandma Lois passed on, her faith lived on through her grandson.

Timothy preached, pastored, and won souls to Christ. What a rich heritage he had! Will we be able to say, "I have taught thee in the way of wisdom; I have led thee in right paths?" *(Prov. 4:11)* What kind of spiritual heritage are we leaving our children? Our influence will live on long after we are gone. With God's help, let's endeavor to make it a good one like Lois and Eunice did.

Lois' roles

1. Mother
2. Grandmother
3. Teacher

Lois' character traits

1. Faithfulness
2. Diligence
3. Persistence

Eunice's roles

1. Wife
2. Mother
3. Widow?
4. Teacher

Eunice's character traits

1. Faithfulness
2. Submissiveness
3. Obedience
4. Wisdom

Sources

Bennett, Richard, and Buckingham, Martin. *Far From Rome, Near to God.* Carlisle, PA: The Banner of Truth Trust, 1997.

Chappell, Clovis G. *Feminine Faces.* Nashville: Abdingdon-Cokesbury Press (Whitmore & Stone), 1942.

Chiniquy, Charles. *Fifty Years in the "Church" of Rome.* Chino, CA: Chick Publications, 1985.

Davis Dictionary of the Bible. Nashville: Royal Publishers, Inc., 1973.

Deen, Edith. *All of the Women of the Bible.* New York: Harper and Row Publishers, 1955.

Deen, Edith. *Wisdom From Women in the Bible.* San Francisco: Harper and Row Publishers, Inc., 1978.

Fallows, Samuel. *The Popular & Critical Bible Encyclopedia*, Vol. I, II, and III. Chicago: The Howard-Severance Company, 1907.

George, Elizabeth. *Women Who Loved God.* Eugene, Oregon: Harvest House Publishers, 1999.

Handford, Elizabeth Rice. *Profiles of Genesis Women.* Chattanooga: Joyful Christian Ministries, 1991.

Handford, Elizabeth Rice. *Women in the Wilderness.* Chattanooga: Joyful Christian Ministries, 1992.

Henry, Matthew. *Matthew Henry's Commentary*, Vol. I and V, Fleming H. Revell Company.

Horton, Robert F. *Women of the Old Testament.* London: Service and Paton, 1899.

Sources (continued)

James, John A. *Female Piety*. Morgan, PA: Soli Deo Gloria Publications, 1994. (reprint from 1860)

Jensen, Mary E. *Bible Women Speak to Us Today*. Minneapolis: Augsburg Publishing House, 1983.

Karssen, Gien. *Her Name is Woman*, Books 1 & 2. Colorado Springs: Navpress, 1991.

Kuyper, Abraham. *Women of the New Testament*. Grand Rapids: Zondervan Publishing House, 1934 (renewed 1962).

Landorf, Joyce. *He Began With Eve*. Word, Inc., 1983.

Lockyer, Herbert. *All the Women of the Bible*. Grand Rapids: Zondervan Publishing House.

Matheson, George. *Portraits of Bible Women*. Grand Rapids: Kregel Publications, 1986.

McAllister, Grace. *God Portrays Women*. Chicago: Moody Press, 1954.

McGee, J. Vernon. *Through the Bible With J. Vernon McGee*. Nashville: Thomas Nelson, Inc., 1981.

Morton, H.V. *Women of the Bible*. New York: Dodd, Mead, and Company, 1941.

Nave, Orville J. *Nave's Topical Bible*. McLean, Virginia: MacDonald Publishing Company.

Orr, James. *The International Standard Bible Encyclopedia*. Grand Rapids: Wm. B. Erdman's Publishing Co., 1939, 1956.

Poole, Matthew. *A Commentary on the Holy Bible*. McLean, Virginia: MacDonald Publishing Company.

Sources (continued)

Price, Eugenia. *God Speaks to Women Today*. Grand Rapids: Zondervan Publishing House, 1964.

Rice, John R. *Genesis –In The Beginning*. Murfreesboro Tennessee: Sword of the Lord Publishers, 1975.

Ryrie, Charles Caldwell. *The Ryrie Study Bible*. Chicago: Moody Press, 1978.

Unger, Merrill F. *Unger's Bible Dictionary*. Chicago: Moody Press, 1966.

Vine, W.E., Merrill F. Unger, and William White, Jr. *Vine's Expository Dictionary of Biblical Words*. Nashville, Camden, New York: Thomas Nelson Publishers, 1985. in America, 1954.

Voss, Carroll. *Women of the Old Testament*. Philadelphia: Women's Missionary Society of the United Lutheran Church in America, 1954.

Webster's Dictionary. Miami: P.S. I. Associates, 1986 ed.

Zodhiates, Spiros Th.D., *The Complete Word Study New Testament*. Chattanooga: AMG Publishers, 1991.

Other Books from Starr Publications

Books by Shirley M. Starr

ABC Character Stories
A Taste of Honey
Dress – A Reflection of the Heart
Family Traditions
Grandma's Touch
Harmony in the Home
Clouds of Adversity—Valleys of Despair
Rescue 911 –Spiritual Diseases
Grace Through Grief   *-diary of loss of granddaughter*
Laugh With Lucy
The Place   *–a 365 day devotional*
The Women of the Bible, volumes 1-5
  Vol. 1 Eve, Sarah, Rachel, Leah, Jochebed, the Virtuous woman, Mary, Elisabeth, Lois, Eunice
  Vol. 2 Rahab, Jael, Ruth, Mary, Martha, Mary Magdalene, Dorcas, Rhoda, Lydia, Priscilla, Phebe
  Vol. 3 Hagar, Dinah, Jephthah's daughter, Naomi, Hannah, Rizpah, Tamar, widow of Zarephath, more
  Vol. 4 Miriam, Deborah, Abigail, Bathsheba, Queen of Sheba, Huldah, Vashti, Esther, Anna, more
  Vol. 5 Lot's wife, Rebekah, Zipporah, Delilah, Michal, Jezebel, Athalia, Herodias, Salome, more

Books by Randy J. Starr

32 Family Devotions, v. 1
The Cancer Earthquake
End Time Events, v. 1   The Rapture
End Time Events, v. 2   The Judgment Seat of Christ & Marriage Supper
Gifts of the Spirit
The Men of the Bible, v. 1   Adam, Cain, Abel, Noah, Nimrod, Melchizedek, and Job
The Prayers of Christ
The Bible Answer Series
  Vol. 1 *The Head Covering*
  Vol. 2 *Tattoos, Body Piercings, & Cuttings*
  Vol. 3 *Drinking*
  Vol. 4 *Gambling*
  Vol. 5 *Speaking in Tongues*

Books by William Hardecker, Jr.

Disciplines of the New Believer   *-8 week devotional for new believer*
Living for and Rejoicing in Christ   *-Study of book of Philippians*
#ToTT (Think on These Things)   -365 day Thought for day daily reader
Answers at a Glance   -Tool to help soul winners and personal workers

3 WAYS TO ORDER

1. On Website: www.starr-publications.com

- **For Ebooks,** click blue bar for Randy's books in Ebook Format or Shirley's books in Ebook Format.

- **For books by other authors,** click Online Store; choose author.

- **For SP books, click Online Store & "Buy Our Books Now"**
  (There will be several pages of books; see bottom to choose page #)

- **To order online with your credit card,**
  Click on any book, choose quantity you want & click & "Add to Bag." When finished ordering, go to checkout and complete your order.

Other ways to ORDER

2. Order Form
On website, click "How to Order" and print our Printable Order Form. Then, mail in your order with a check.

3. Phone
CALL (717) 309-6384 to order with your credit card.

———————————

We look forward to hearing from you.

 Starr Publications
754 E Main St.
Dallastown, PA 17313

When you see Starr Publications on the outside,
you can trust what's on the inside!

* *

If you are a Pastor and would like Randy and Shirley Starr
to come to your church, call us or find more info at:

www.starr-ministries.com